A Child Who Felt Too Much

& Other Therapeutic Tales of Love and Healing For The New Millennium

Roger Keizerstein

Published by Dahlitz Media Pty Ltd
ISBN: 978-0-9944080-4-4

Cover image by Andriyko Podilnyk
https://unsplash.com/photos/eL0APgBYcqY

DEDICATION

For my mother, Mildred Ginsberg Keizerstein, whose fierce commitment to my development as a writer and person, made the creation of this book possible.

CONTENTS

Acknowledgments   i

Foreword   ii

1   A Child Who Felt Too Much   1
2   19-year-old Tyler Overcomes Paralyzing Social Anxiety   15
3   Four-year-old Domingo Resolves Trauma Through Art   29
4   Through Illness A Veteran Faces and Overcomes his Painful Past   41
5   32-year-old Melissa Triumphs Over Complex Trauma   52
6   Carl And Cecilia Revisited   81
7   Treatment of a 12-Year-old Boy With Trauma   96

ACKNOWLEDGMENTS

I would like to thank my friend, colleague and editor, Samuel Taube, for his steadfast guidance and attention to detail, that brought the enclosed case studies to life.

Also, Joseph Reiher and Prudence Emery, of the Nassau County Chapter of the New York State Society of Clinical Social Workers, who invited me to speak on trauma and post-traumatic stress and published my first explorations on the topic in their newsletter.

Great thanks and gratitude to the publisher of the Science Of Psychotherapy Magazine, Matthew Dahlitz and its wonderful editor Richard Hill, for publishing all my case studies, although they read more like short stories, then the typical clinical studies.

Last, but not least, I would like to thank my sister Holly McClean, who supported and enthusiastically encouraged my early efforts at writing and typed many of the stories I so earnestly produced during my teen years.

These case studies were originally published in *The Neuropsychotherapist* and *The Science of Psychotherapy* magazine, between August 2018 and July 2021 – https://thescienceofpsychotherapy.com

FOREWORD

When I was a young and earnest therapist, my training and my own analysis, placed an emphasis on objectivity and personal anonymity. A therapist was not to inject his subjective views into the therapy, divulge personal information to the client and god forbid, show emotion. To quote Sigmund Freud "Don't trust yourself, don't trust your patient, only trust the process." For years I struggled to comply with Freud's dictum with varying degrees of success.

In the early 1990's, about 12 years into my practice, I was sitting across from the parent of a child I had been working with for nearly nine years. Her child, Tamara, had been born with fetal alcohol syndrome and had struggled with a slew of behavior, learning and speech impediments. She was now an 18-year-old high school senior, working part-time at a supermarket and planning on furthering her education at a local community college that specialized in the hotel and hospitality business.

Tamara's mother and I were discussing a payment issue—her new health insurance company was balking at paying for sessions on some arcane technicality.

"I was talking to a woman at the insurance company, and she said you were so nice and pleasant on the phone, unlike the irate therapists she often has to deal with."

I chuckled. "I speak softly. But don't carry a big stick."

She laughed. "She was so impressed by your manner that she wanted to know all about you, personal things. It suddenly dawned on me that I couldn't tell her anything because I didn't know any more than she did."

I suddenly felt flush with embarrassment.

"Are you married? Do you have children? Do you live nearby?"

I smiled. "I am married. And I hope to have children. And I live in the city."

After some chit-chat, I paused, leaned forward, put my hands together and looked up. "Although you know so little about me personally, and I know so much about you, and that seems odd and possibly unfair, I can assure you that I love your daughter and all the children I work with; and I am committed to their welfare without reservation."

"I know," she nodded, her eyes misting. "I know."

It is likely that Tamara's mother believed that what I meant by "I love your daughter," had to do with how I felt toward her, *feelings* I just didn't show. On this point she would be partly right. But If Tamara's therapy was dependent on how I felt toward her, it would likely fail, like so many marriages that come to an end because someone "fell out of love."

What I actually meant by love had more to do with creating the conditions in Tamara's life from which she could grow and develop inside and outside of my office. In my play therapy room, Tamara was able to express—at times, re-enact—scenes from her conflict riven home life and as a result, temper the emotions roiling inside her. Playing "teacher," she could give shape and order to the frustration she so often felt being constantly asked to repeat herself because her speech was so easily misunderstood. Outside my office, at school district meetings, I fought to prevent committees on special education from placing her in educational programs far from home or in classrooms filled with boys with severe behavior problems. Thus, the love I speak of, although it does have a degree of feeling at its core, had more to do with the way in which I interacted with Tamara and those in her therapeutic and educational orbit.

Like the word love, the word healing, *to heal*, occupies an important place in the therapeutic vernacular. I prefer the word healing because it suggests that a client is recovering from injury, rather than being treated for a "disorder." The school district and the psychologists that evaluated Tamara, often referred to her as being "disturbed" or "disordered" in their reports, and subsequently she was perceived by new teachers as being "out of control," before they even met her.

To label Tamara disturbed or disordered was not only unkind— *unloving*—but unscientific because it implied that Tamara was complicit in her own emotional dysregulation, when in actuality, her various challenges were the result of an injury she suffered in utero, due to her once addicted mother's consumption of alcohol. If I would have also viewed Tamara as disturbed or disordered--conspired in her objectification—it would have placed her at an emotional distance from me that would have likely lead to therapeutic failure.

Similarly, the individuals in the following seven case studies are not suffering from disorders, but rather from various psychic injuries. Patrick, a hypersensitive child, had been injured not only by overstimulation but also by being taunted and bullied by peers due to his perceived "unrelatedness." Adding insult to injury, an army of helping professionals simply didn't, perhaps couldn't, understand Patrick, distressing him further, because the clinical lens through which they were viewing him was too narrow.

Then there's Colin, Domingo and Melissa, all suffering from various forms of trauma and post-traumatic stress. Remarkedly, many in the mental health field continue to refer to those suffering from the symptoms of trauma, post-traumatic stress, as a disorder, PTSD. The symptoms of post-traumatic stress (PTS) are a result of injury to the nervous system, the autonomic nervous system (ANS), not a disorder. The D in (PTSD) should be replaced with the letter I for "Injury"(PTSI) not merely because calling PTS a disorder is unnecessarily stigmatizing, but scientifically untrue, as I will demonstration in great detail in some of the case studies to follow.

A CHILD WHO FELT TOO MUCH

Too often, when a child presents with certain behaviors, styles of communicating and relating to others that lend themselves to quick categorization, we lose sight of who the child really is. Subsequently, a diagnosis is arrived at prematurely, and an adverse treatment plan is ushered into place.

Conversely, it is the job of the practitioner to see into the uniqueness of every child that comes into his or her care. Through careful, patient observation and consultation with those within the child's social sphere, the grander picture of the child will emerge with all its relevant nuance.

I began to work with Patrick and his family when he was a six-year-old. Patrick was a handsome blonde-haired child who had received early intervention services as a preschooler. The services he received—speech and occupational therapy and special education support—belied the developmental history I received from his parents during our initial interview. Besides breaking a leg at eight months old, Patrick's developmental history was uneventful. He had met all milestones within normal range. Why than had he received so many services?

"Patrick has unusual reactions to music and singing and other noises—especially sudden noises," Patrick's mother, Kathy, explained.

"What kind of sudden noises?"

"An air conditioner going on or off, a space heater."

"I see," I replied.

"And don't forget thunder and lighting," Patrick's father, Arthur, added. "He becomes petrified. He races for his bed covers or locks himself in the bathroom."

"It sounds like he's seeking shelter," I said sympathetically. "Safety."

At first, Kathy and Arthur seemed surprised by my answer, but eventually nodded in agreement.

I purposely referred to Patrick's "unusual" reactions, especially to thunder and lightning, as a resource, a way to protect himself. This non-judgmental perspective also served to give Patrick's parents a glimpse into how I viewed a child's attempt to cope with his environment, especially if he was experiencing moments of sensory over-stimulation, or "sensory overload."

"What happens in the classroom when music is played or when children sing?"

"He becomes overwhelmed. He covers his ears and insists they stop."

"I'm sure that goes over really well with his teachers," I joked.

"Yeah, right." Kathy frowned sarcastically. "He hasn't even entered the first grade and they already see him as a pain in the you-know-what."

Kathy was exactly right. Patrick's perceived belligerence—his insistence that music and singing lessons be stopped on his behalf—was more of a concern to his teachers than his apparent oversensitivity to certain sounds and is what prompted the school's psychologist to refer him to me for psychotherapeutic services.

"So that I understand this correctly," I said. "Patrick's unusual reactions—or put somewhat differently—his over-sensitivities—is what the school believes is interfering with his academic and social progress? Hence, all the services."

"Exactly," Kathy replied.

When I spoke to Patrick's teacher and the school's psychologist, I received a slightly different perspective on his behavior and how they were adjusting to it.

His kindergarten teacher had decided to accommodate Patrick's sensitivity to music and singing by giving him the option of leaving the classroom before the lesson began. "Yet this didn't stop him from insisting that we not play music or sing on his behalf." The teacher chuckled. "But we can go so far."

The school's psychologist, who had observed Patrick a few times in the classroom and also had conducted a few play therapy sessions with him, added, "Patrick is not only over sensitive to many classroom activities, but seems socially adrift, outside the group, mostly playing by himself. He appears at times to be unrelated."

"Are you considering a classification of Asperger's Syndrome?" I asked.

"We have. But we'll leave that up to you and Patrick's parents."

"Thank you," I replied. "You've been very informative, very helpful."

My first few sessions with Patrick did render a profile of a child whose style of play and relating suggested an Asperger-like adaptation. He made little eye contact, even while talking, thus the occasional, yet sudden sweep into view of his beautiful blue eyes was arresting. He did not play interactively, preferring to construct farms and small villages from Lincoln Logs and large Lego bricks of blue and white. Patrick played with the same toys over and over again, ignoring or politely turning away my overtures to join him.

Since I adhered strictly to the criteria for Asperger's Syndrome established by Dr. Hans Asperger in 1944, I determined that Patrick was a hypersensitive child with Asperger-like features. For him to have fit the classical Asperger profile, he would have needed to have a history of arm-flapping or rocking or episodic (inexplicable) screaming for long periods of time; he'd also have had to demonstrate a recurring fixation on the parts of things, rather than their function; and he'd have to be socially-impaired—unable to pick up on social cues, rather than being socially reticent. Some hypersensitive children, not all, look askance while speaking or being spoken to, better to manage the sensory experience and to concentrate on and process what is being said.

Subsequently, I played alongside Patrick, periodically commenting on what he was doing and what I was doing as well. Parallel play and labeling— creating a shared narrative between child and therapist, *a memory of therapy sessions*—is an excellent way of communicating to a child that you accept, unconditionally, his style of play and relating, and that you are in tune with who he is and where he's at emotionally, even if you're seemingly "interacting" very little. These early, simple therapeutic interventions can cultivate the ground upon which more substantial work can take place as the child reaches more mature emotional and cognitive developmental levels.

Over the next few years my work with Patrick was multifaceted. I had weekly play therapy sessions with him; bimonthly parenting sessions with his mother; and monthly consultations with his teachers and the school's psychologist.

Sessions with Patrick rendered slow, incremental steps of progress: his play became more varied, and our eyes met more often, especially when we played board games such as *Candy Land*, *Sorry* and *Guess Who*. His unusual reactions to music and singing began to fade, as did his over sensitivity to other forms of external stimuli. He also formed a close friendship with a younger boy who moved in next door. Patrick, along with his younger brother Steven, and their new friend, often played together in each other's homes, demonstrating on Patrick's part a developing ability to manage transitions and environments other than his own. It appeared that Patrick was beginning to naturally modulate incoming stimuli in a way that tempered the anxiety it previously triggered and restricted his movement. Nonetheless, Patrick remained remote and seemingly inattentive in class and had fallen behind academically by as much as a year and the half. But since he scored within average range on a battery of tests administered by the school's psychologist, Patrick didn't qualify for any special education services.

Since Patrick's mother Kathy was a stay-at-home mom, she was the one mostly involved, compared with his father, who worked full-time. Subsequently, I got to know her well and was able to get a more detailed picture of her family background.

Kathy grew up in a large, conflict riven, Irish Catholic family in which material and emotional resources were in small supply. Her parents worked long hours and she and her siblings were often left to fend for themselves. By junior high, Kathy had taken on a maternal role in an attempt to create a modicum of order in the household, cooking and cleaning and making sure her younger siblings' schoolwork was done. Subsequently, Kathy's siblings grew to depend on her and resent her in equal measure.

"Anytime I get involved in the care of my parents, my younger brother and sister get all defensive. It causes all types of unnecessary drama."

"How come?" I asked.

"I think they perceive me as over-bearing, taking over, instead of helping out."

From my vantage point, Kathy *could* be perceived as being over-bearing, *bossy*, because of the emotional intensity and seriousness that she brought to her interactions with others, especially regarding the care of her parents and her children. Kathy was very direct, *didn't pull any punches*, and was as articulate as a seasoned lawyer.

"I just want things done right. I want people to pay attention to details."

"I understand," I said. "Attention to details is important."

But there was another, less positive aspect to Kathy's emotional intensity. She tended to imbue Patrick's missteps and short-term regressions, with greater intensity than warranted. When Patrick failed a test, received a poor report card, or had another emotional meltdown in school, she often responded with alarm.

"This is disastrous," she'd say. "When is he ever going to catch up? When is he ever going to stop having these emotional breakdowns?"

"I can understand your concern," I'd start off by saying. "But let's look at the big picture."

I would procced to describe in detail the progress Patrick had made since the beginning of his therapy and point out the discrepancy between his academic performance and social behavior in school and what she and others saw at home.

"You're right,' Kathy acknowledged. "He's a much different child at home, and we are pleased with his progress."

"I see the changes in my office as well. As long as we provide Patrick with ongoing support and accept him for who he is, "quirks" and all, he'll come along. These are obstacles to overcome, not impediments."

"I love him so much." Kathy smiled through misty eyes. "Quirks and all."

"I do too."

When a parent reacts to a child's apparent "failure" with great emotional intensity, it is incumbent upon the therapist not to react in kind. Conversely, responding in a calm, reassuring manner, models emotional regulation in the face of stress and helps a parent manage the ups and downs of their child's life more realistically, much more effectively. The child psychoanalyst D.W. Winnicott, refers to this as the "holding environment" where the therapist keeps the feelings of the client in place—avoids escalation—and acts in a calm and comforting manner.

Regarding Patrick's teachers and the school's psychologist, I responded calmly and confidently to their ongoing concerns about Patrick's lack of progress academically and socially and their recommendation that he receive a medication evaluation for his distractibility and occasional emotional meltdowns.

"I don't think he needs a medication evaluation at this time," I'd tell them.

"But he's still way behind," they'd counter.

"In school, I'd agree. But outside of school he's much more focused— notice how consistently he does his homework and completes assignments. Also, he has a close friend or two on his block."

"What about another try at special ed? Maybe he could get an outside eval? The school would have to comply with its findings until they did their own, if they decided to challenge it at all."

"I'll pass on your suggestion to Patrick's parents."

Patrick attended school in a district with which I had a long, cooperative relationship. I received a year of training at the district 35 years earlier. Subsequently, I have been a primary referral source ever since. But most of the professionals that I had collaborated with over three decades earlier had retired. The new staff of teachers, social workers and psychologists were quick to recommend medication for all kinds of maladies, particularly those that purported to improve a child's ability to concentrate and/or control his impulses.

In Patrick's case, his "distractibility" or seeming inattentiveness in the classroom was not a result of an inability to focus on subject matter that did not hold his interest. Nor was it related to an inability to overcome boredom. It was, however, his attempt to manage a large-group, classroom sensory experience. Hypersensitivity of all kinds, whether it be an over-reaction to visual, auditory or tactile stimulation or combinations of any of the three, is likely, from a neuroscientific perspective, amygdala based. The amygdala, part of the brain's limbic system, is not only responsible for the processing of fear, but it alerts an individual to present danger—it's a threat detector. Any attempt to tamper with or worse yet tranquilize through medication an individual's threat detector, *their ability to perceive and survive life-threatening confrontations*, however well-meaning, is a fool hearty endeavor at best.

When Patrick was 12 years old, the summer before he was to begin junior high, he came into my office and said, "My parents want me to discuss something with you. It's a bit embarrassing."

"Take your time," I replied. "I'm all ears."

Patrick took a deep breath.

"I'm kind of afraid of thunder and lightning. When it happens, I feel overwhelmed with fear. I run into the bathroom, turn off the light, wait till it's over."

"It seems as if you feel a need to protect yourself."

"That's one way of looking at it." Patrick was slumped over, and his face was pale.

"Well, people seek all kinds of ways of protecting themselves when they're afraid, some ways more obvious than others. You're not alone in this."

Patrick looked up. "I didn't *think* I was. But at times it sure *feels* like it."

Hypersensitive children often do not identify with their peers emotionally because they process external stimuli, *have sensory experiences*, that are far more intense. When other children do not react with nearly the same intensity to the same phenomenon—music, singing or to thunder and lightning, to name a few— children such as Patrick do not see themselves reflected in others. The great irony is hypersensitive children are often accused of not having empathy for others because they appear to feel too little, when in actuality it's because they feel too much.

"Could I ask you a question about how you protect yourself from thunder and lightning?"

"You might as well."

"Why the bathroom? Why do you seek shelter there?"

"The bathroom doesn't have a window and it's the smallest room in the house. It's got a room in back of it and a room in front of it."

"More protection?"

"I think so."

I took a sip from my mug of tea. Patrick gulped down some water from a small bottle of Poland Spring.

"Are there any other sounds that compel you to seek cover?"

"Not anymore. But as you know, I used to get easily startled when I was younger."

"Right. I do remember." I said. "So, you don't react similarly to sirens, heavy metal music, a house alarm?"

"No. Not anymore than anyone else."

Patrick gulped down some more water. His breathing appeared to be steadier, and the color had returned to his face. Thus, I decided to continue on with my line of questioning to explore, if only indirectly, his reaction to thunder and lightning.

"Have you ever heard of the brain's Fear Center?" I asked.

"Vaguely. Something on PBS."

I chuckled. "Yes. It's very in vogue nowadays, often in the news."

Patrick's laughter was slightly delayed, but its tone did communicate why he thought I was laughing: (all that crazy science stuff on PBS).

"Do you know what it is?"

Patrick shook his head.

"Well, it's a place in the brain that triggers the fear response and accounts for why people react to things differently. Why one person can't tolerate the sound of a house alarm or the sight of a chicken or a clown on stilts or odors emanating from a cow's you know what." Patrick was now laughing. "You'd be surprised by what triggers the response."

"But the Fear Center also detects a special kind of fear, the type that activates the threat alarm in the brain and compels a person to seek shelter. This is what happens to you in the face of thunder and lightning."

The expression on Patrick's face seemed to suggest that he was beginning to understand what I was saying.

"Why is it that you do not feel threatened by loud music or the sound of a house alarm. Why do you not seek shelter from these sounds? Do you have any idea why?"

"A house alarm can't hurt me. It can be turned off. But lightning *can* hurt me, and I can't control it in any way."

"Great insight, Patrick!" His face was beaming. "You're absolutely right. The issue is not being afraid per se, but not having any control over what you're afraid of. That trips the threat alarm."

Hypersensitive children, due to sensory overload, especially during early childhood, seek control of their environments to cope with and manage their internal states. This defensive posture is too often misinterpreted by well-meaning parents and teachers—and even mental health professionals—as a form of disobedience, defiant behavior. This couldn't be further from the truth. It's actually a child's attempt to temper their rising emotional thermostat. Once this is understood by all concerned and strategically accommodated, hypersensitive children often blossom into socially empathetic, creative teenagers, not in spite of their propensity toward sensory overload, but because of it.

Two sessions later, I decided to encourage Patrick to continue to explore his fear of thunder and lightning, in the hope that he might incorporate a few stress- response exercises into his daily routine. This would be an indirect way of possibly helping him reduce the intensity of his reaction to thunder and lightning, a method of desensitizing the area of his brain discussed earlier, that was being triggered, the amygdala.

"I've been working on a method of helping children and teens reduce stress. All kinds of stress. Taking a test in school. Trying out for the basketball team. Or coping with a parent or sibling being sick."

Patrick nodded.

"Can you think of any stressful situations?"

"Asking out a girl?"

"Now that would be really stressful."

We both laughed.

"My method is called the one plus two plus three equals six sequence. Can you say it out loud? One plus two plus three equals six?"

Patrick was giggling. "One plus two plus three equals six."

"One more time."

"One plus two plus three equals six."

"Very good."

"What are you trying to do, hypnotize me?"

"Hmmm---" I reached for Patrick's file, took out a pen. "Hypnotize Patrick next week to get him to reveal the winning lottery numbers."

Patrick was now laughing hard.

I put Patrick's file back and put the pen in my shirt pocket.

"Ok," I smiled. "This is how it works." I stood up. "One represents my head," I touched my head. "Two represents my heart." I touched my heart. "And three represents my body." I tapped my thighs and legs and feet.

"So, what's in your head?"

Patrick was laughing again. "Your brain?"

"I hope so," I laughed. "But what does your brain do?"

"Think?"

"That's right. So, what's in your head are thoughts."

"What's in your heart?"

"Feelings."

"Right. What's down here?" I ran my hands over my lower limbs.

"Your body."

"Right. The rest of your body."

"So, one represents thoughts, two represents feelings, and three represents your body."

"I get it." Patrick nodded.

"When you respond to thunder and lightning and you're in the bathroom, what number are you on?"

Patrick at first seemed perplexed by the question, then cupped his chin in his hand and leaned over, apparently thinking it over. "Zero. I'm frozen."

"Precisely." I leaned over slightly and titled my head rightward. "Would you like *not* to be frozen?"

"Yes." Patrick was firm in his reply.

"Ok. Would it be all right if you sit on the couch, get as comfortable as you can and close your eyes? All kidding aside, I am not going to hypnotize you."

Patrick sat back on the couch, moved his legs into a comfortable position, let his arms fall limp to his sides and closed his eyes.

"Ok. The next time you hear thunder and lightning, I want you to go into the bathroom, close the door, shut off the light and take a seat. Once there, presumably sitting on a closed toilet cover, not the bathtub—" Patrick was giggling. "Try to settle yourself into the comfortable, relaxed position that you're in now."

"O.K.," Patrick's voice was soft.

"Then I want you to say: One are my thoughts. Two are my feelings. Three is the rest of my body. Can you do that now?"

Patrick nodded. "One is my thoughts. Two are my feelings. Three is the rest of my body."

"Very good, Patrick. Very good. How does that feel."

"Good."

"Ok. Please repeat after me. My thought is: I am safe. My feeling is: I am in control. My body is: calm."

"My thought is: I'm safe. My feeling is: I'm in control. My body is: calm."

"Excellent Patrick. Excellent."

Notice, I did not ask Patrick to give up the shelter of the bathroom when thunder and lightning came his way. Why not? Asking Patrick to give up a protective resource at this time might be premature, and lead to therapeutic failure. But while he was in the safe confines of the bathroom, he could use the relaxation technique we practiced in the office. This would help unfreeze him and teach him how to counter the threat-based adrenaline rush triggered by the thunder and lightning; an adrenaline rush that put him on the **fast track to the amygdala**. The one plus two plus three equals six sequence slowed down the entire process, promoted deliberate thinking and provided Patrick with a method of modulating his emotional responses to frightening sensory input and improve his stress responses overall.

Although I lived 50 miles from my office, when dark ominous clouds circled overhead, threatening to erupt in thunder and emit thin shards of lighting that lit and electrified the sky, I couldn't help but think of Patrick. What if it happened when he was in school? What if he was home alone? Would he apply the relaxation techniques we practiced in my office? Would he even remember what to do? Had my interventions been premature? Would they even work? Only time would tell.

During the next two sessions, Patrick and I practiced the one plus two plus three equals six sequence. I also introduced a few more neuroscientific concepts, mostly from Kate Cohen-Posey's Neuroscience For Clinicians Manual.

"Do you like peppermint?" I asked.

"Yes. Sometimes my mom and I have peppermint tea at night. It's supposed to help you sleep."

"Right. One brand is Sleepytime Peppermint Tea."

"I think we have that."

"Do you know why it helps you sleep?"

"Not exactly. But I know it works."

"Well..." I smiled. "Peppermint is a muscle relaxer. And when your muscles are relaxed it's easier to fall asleep."

"That makes sense."

"But there's another very important aspect to this. Why would peppermint, of all things, promote a relaxed bodily state?"

"I have no idea," Patrick replied.

"Peppermint is made up of the ingredient, Menthol. Menthol switches on a part of the brain that tells the body to relax, promoting a state of calm. That part of the brain is called the parasympathetic nervous system. You might learn about it in Biology class when you move on to the high school."

"Sounds interesting."

I took out a sheet of paper with the heading, **To Prevent Panic Attacks And Ease All Forms of Anxiety**. It listed 14 ways of going from an anxious state to a calm one. I handed it to Patrick. "Please look at number Seven. Can you read it to me?"

"Suck on a peppermint Altoid," Patrick started to giggle. "Hold it against the roof of your mouth with your tongue. This can also cause salivating and swallowing."

"Thank you. Now read from the column next to it."

"Sucking, salivating and swallowing all turn on the 9th brainstem rest-connect nerve (PSNS). Peppermint relaxes muscles."

"Do you know what PSNS stands for?"

"Not a clue."

"The parasympathetic nervous system. The part of the brain I referred to before. The one that tells the body to relax, to be calm, at ease."

"I'll have to study this to remember."

"Even, or especially at 13 years old, it'll be well worth your time."

Patrick and I went over two other easy to employ relaxation techniques, a small bottle of cold water to the forehead or face and counting by threes backwards from a hundred. "These methods all do them same thing. They turn on the parasympathetic nervous system, helping a person transition from an anxious state to a calm one."

I decided against providing Patrick with a tutorial on the sympathetic nervous system, the part of the brain where feelings (stress and anxiety) are located and the fact that the sympathetic and parasympathetic nervous systems are actually two branches of the larger autonomic nervous system. I thought that providing Patrick with too much information might serve to confuse him and possibly undermine the objective of teaching him how to modulate his feeling states, to manage more intimately his bodily sensations.

As often happens in the Northeastern region of the United States during the fall season, thunder and lightning rein down, as the days grow shorter and winter approaches. Anytime dark, ominous clouds gathered overhead, wherever I might be, I couldn't help but think of Patrick. How would he react? Would he employ the relaxation techniques we practiced in the office?

In between sessions, Patrick's mother telephoned. "He didn't go in the bathroom. He just stayed in his room."

"Oh," I said, finally realizing what Kathy was talking about. "During last night's thunder and lightning show?"

"Yes." Kathy was whispering. "I guess he'll talk to you about it tomorrow."

"I look forward to it."

"Thank you." Kathy said softly, her voice filled with emotion.

"You're welcome."

The next afternoon, Patrick came into my office and immediately sat down on the couch opposite me. I purposely busied myself, brewing a cup of tea. "Would you like some tea?"

"No thanks," he replied. "Did my mother call you?"

"Yes. She did."

"Did she tell you what happened?"

"Some. Why don't you fill me in?"

Patrick proceeded to tell me that when the thunder and lightning came, he was sitting at his desk in his room. Instead of retreating to the bathroom, he decided to lie back on his bed, close his eyes and employ the one plus two plus three equals six sequence. He did it three times. "I felt a bit uneasy, hoping the thunder and lightning would soon pass, but I wasn't at all panicky or felt the need to escape to the bathroom. At some point, when I thought the coast was clear, I got up, went into the kitchen and made myself a cup of peppermint tea. An hour later, I was able to eat dinner without any problems."

"That's great Patrick. That's really great." Suddenly gripped by emotion, I took a sip of tea and raised my cup. "Cheers," I smiled. "Cheers."

Armed with the skills to modulate his bodily sensations and effectively manage sensory input, Patrick entered high school with an ability to handle the often, volatile ups and downs of everyday teenage existence, inside and outside of school. He made a group of friends, all oversensitive "quirky types", the kind of friends that might last a lifetime. They communicated all day long with each other by text and email and planned mid-week and weekend outings to the movies, bowling alleys and dinners at a nearby mall. Patrick became the designated peacemaker, helping the group settle disputes, get over hurt feelings, due to their over sensitivities.

Since the early 1990's, I have worked with dozens of hypersensitive children of varying kinds and many of them have grown up to become teachers, graphic artists, engineers and great moms and dads. Patrick, now 17, a child who once felt too much, plans on attending a nearby university and immersing himself in the study of meteorology.

References

Arden, J., (2019). *Mind-Brain-Gene: Toward Psychotherapy Integration*. New York, NY: W.W. Norton & Company.

Aron, E. N., & Aron, A. (1997). Sensory-processing sensitivity and its relation to introversion and emotionality. *Journal of Personality and Social Psychology, 73*(2), 345–368. https://doi.org/10.1037/0022-3514.73.2.345Asperger, Hans, Asperger's Syndrome, Health.Harvard.edu, March 2014.

AUEssays. (November 2018). Holding and Containing - Winnicott (1960). Retrieved from https://www.auessays.com/essays/psychology/holding-and-containing-winnicott.php?vref=1

Axline, V., (1969). *Play Therapy*. New York, NY: Ballantine Books.

Cohen-Posey, K. (2016) *Neuroscience for Clinicians: Brain Change for Anxiety, Trauma, Impulse Control, Depression and Relationships*. PESI digital seminar: https://catalog.pesi.com/item/neuroscience-clinicians-brain-change-anxiety-trauma-impulse-control-depression-relationships-13594

Cozolino, L, (2013). The Fast and Slow Tracks To The Amygdala. In *The Social Neuroscience of Education: Optimizing Attachment and Learning In The Classroom*. New York, NY: W.W. Norton & Company.

Logsdon, A. (2020). Attention Deficit Disorder, Without Hyperactivity, online - https://www.verywellmind.com/add-and-attention-deficit-disorders-2161810

19-YEAR-OLD TYLER OVERCOMES PARALYZING SOCIAL ANXIETY

I met Tyler for the first time when he was nine years old. He was a tense, rigid child with sensory integration impairment.

As usual, I met with his parents beforehand to take a detailed developmental history and an accounting of his presenting problems. Tyler's history rendered a profile of a hypersensitive child with all the classic characteristics (Healy, 2011). He was physically agitated in the hospital nursery and inconsolably colicky at nine months. In play group and preschool, he was unable to share or give up control or transition from one activity to another in an age-appropriate manner, often becoming so agitated and dysregulated that he had to be temporarily separated from the group until he was able to regain his composure. To his parents, Tyler's only saving grace was his intelligence.

"What would you like me to help him with?" I asked.

"We would like for him to learn how to relax, roll with the punches—like other kids. Develop skills to make friends and get along with others."

During our first session, Tyler sat across from me, arms folded across his chest, his face scrunched up, refusing to utter a word. He rejected my offer to do parallel drawing, play a round of Uno, or have at any of the dozen or so board games that stacked the shelves of my office cabinet.

"Just got off from school? Hungry? How about a pack of Oriole Cookies? They're mint!" I exclaimed.

Tyler remained mute.

I retrieved a small bottle of water from my side table. "Poland Spring anyone?" I wanted to say it gets hot in here when you're as angry as a volcano ready to erupt but I didn't.

My attempt to nurture Tyler with food and drink failed miserably and after two or three sessions of this I feared that I was conspiring in the emotional torture of a child who simply found it too disquieting, too painful to accept any more help for his social and emotional difficulties, possibly because it would be admitting to such difficulties, making him intolerably vulnerable and worse yet, affirm the low regard with which he was held by those around him. To preserve whatever self-esteem he still clung to, Tyler chose to win, even by default.

I told Tyler's parents that I would be more than willing to work with them and his teacher to help him learn how to "relax" and socialize with other children more effectively, but until he became more amendable to the therapeutic process, I wouldn't be willing to work with him directly.

"We thought that you would be able to bring him along in time," was their rather terse reply. And I never heard from them again.

At least until ten years later.

At first Tyler's mother had not remembered that she had brought him to see me a decade earlier and neither did I. But as we spoke, and she became more familiar with my office location and my relationship with her school district she remembered that she had brought Tyler in to see me a few times.

"Would you consider seeing him again?" she finally asked.

"Would you consider having me as his therapist?" I joked.

We both had a hearty laugh.

During the last two summers off from college, Tyler had tried two therapists, but they weren't a match and he stopped seeing them after a few sessions.

"Does Tyler want to see a therapist at this time? Is he motivated?"

"He's more like desperate," she replied. "He's now finding it difficult to speak in public."

I agreed to see Tyler. "We'll see how it goes."

"Thank you." Tyler's mother's voice was stressed but full of gratitude for my willingness to take him on.

A week later, a few minutes into what Tyler's scheduled appointment would be, I received a call from his mother. "He's lost. He can't find your office."

"Text me his phone number. Let him know that I'll be calling him soon."

I put on my head set and walked outside and started toward the main road. "Tyler. This is Roger. Your mom tells me you're having trouble finding my office. It happens all the time. There are two Brewster Lanes. I apologize for not giving you a proper heads-up."

Tyler was able to tell me his exact location. "Very good," I tried to sound upbeat. "I'll guide you every step of the way."

When I saw his car approach from the main road, I waved him into the office parking lot. Forgetting that I no longer needed to talk to him by phone I said.

"No worries, Tyler. You'll have a full session. Meet you inside."

Once back in my office I texted my next client that I was running about 15 minutes late.

I took this opportunity to model for Tyler a calm, emotionally regulated reaction to stress, i.e., being late for your first therapy appointment. I also wanted to impress upon him that my interpersonal style as a therapist and "regular guy" was non-judgmental and flexible, accommodating.

After shaking my hand firmly, Tyler sat across from me on the couch, lifted his head slightly and said, "By the way, you did give me a heads up. I just didn't read the text carefully." He was referring to the text message I had sent him a few days before.

"Well," I smiled, pausing momentarily, "You're here."

"I'm here," Tyler nodded.

I took out my notebook and said. "Usually, the first time around I ask a lot of questions, take some notes. It that all right?"

"Sure," Tyler said.

Tyler, nearly 20, had spent the last two years studying engineering at a college far from home. Although his grades were good, he was unhappy there from the start. According to Tyler it was a "crummy" looking dormitory at a state school, dark, cold and snowy six months a year. Worse yet, almost all his dorm mates were science and engineering students, mostly introverts, with little interpersonal skills and there were few casual ways in which to meet young woman unless he was willing to leave his comfort zone and trapeze across campus or head into town.

"Just curious." I said. "How come you stayed?"

"Never thought you'd ask?" I think this was Tyler's attempt at sarcasm.

"My damn parents made me. First it was stick it out, you'll get used to it, make friends.

Then it was 'you can't leave now. You're halfway through your degree. Screw that."

"So, you're not returning?"

"Hell no. Even if I have to drop out of school all together."

"Are you?"

Tyler shook his head smiling. "No. My parents finally gave in. I'll be going to a school locally this fall."

Tyler had a job at a local pizza place, taking orders, occasionally waiting tables, making deliveries.

"The money's good, but the job is real nerve wracking. I told my boss that I would rather just take orders, so I don't have to deal with too many people."

"I see," I nodded. "Uh, your mother told me over the phone that you're having some difficulties speaking in public. Is that accurate? You seem fine talking here."

"Yeah." Tyler looked up at me. "I freeze. I just can't get the words out. I can actually feel myself turning red."

"In light of the fact that you spent two years in a dormitory practically talking to no one, you're a bit rusty. But I can assure you that I can help you overcome this, and you will leave here today with tools to begin that process."

"Thank you." Tyler's eyes misted up.

Let me offer some background on Tyler's symptoms.

When a person freezes to a point where that can't speak, especially when there isn't a medically related reason, they are likely experiencing something called parasympathetic impairment and in Tyler's case freeze (Amlie, 2018). The autonomic nervous system (ANS) is responsible for managing stress and the modulation of states or levels of anxiety. The ANS has two branches: The sympathetic nervous system and the parasympathetic nervous system. The sympathetic nervous system detects levels of threat and communicates those threats to our bodies in extremis, the part of the brain called the Amygdala, to keep us safe (Dahlitz, 2017). The parasympathetic nervous system functions to provide equilibrium and homeostasis and calm to the entire system. When the ANS is working effectively the sympathetic nervous system detects threats when they exist; and the parasympathetic nervous system engenders homeostasis when you should be calm.

Conversely, when the ANS is impaired, then something as simple as saying "Hello," "Thank you," "You're welcome," or looking someone in the eye, and for that matter, presenting yourself with an upright posture, can become exceedingly difficult. High level parasympathetic functioning puts the body in a state of what is referred to by neurologists as "rest and digest," when it's easy to breath and to eat. Conversely, if you're always feeling nervous and dreadful and slumped over in a defensive posture, your breathing will be impeded, and you'll be predisposed to a state of body tightness and a feeling akin to being on the verge of regurgitating.

To provide Tyler with a path to bringing his ANS back into balance, I would have to find a series of what the neuropsychotherapist Matthew Dahlitz refers to as "sweet spots" (2017). A sweet spot is a place where a highly anxious person—whose sympathetic nervous system is overwrought—is challenged to move out of his or her comfort zone in small, manageable ways, but not overwhelmed by the experience.

"So, tell me," I said. "How do things go at work? Describe your day."

"I usually get there at three, hope my boss doesn't ask me to do deliveries, and get right to work. It's a busy popular place."

"Do you interact with your co-workers?"

"As little as possible. I put my head down and do my work. I get in and out as soon as I can. Some days it exhausts me just being there."

"O.K." I said. "Here's some homework."

I sat upright in my chair and said. "Do you think it would be too much for you to enter the pizza place with an upright posture and a smile on your face?"

"No." Tyler sounded a note of sarcasm.

"And could you make good eye contact with your co-workers and say hello?"

Tyler nodded affirmatively.

"And when you leave say good-bye?"

"Yes." Tyler sounded like he was getting it.

"This way you can begin to reverse the impression that you've been giving your co-workers—which is what?"

"That I don't like them." Tyler got misty eyed again.

I left a tender moment alone. "See you next week."

I opened our next session by asking Tyler, "How'd your week go?"

Tyler leaned over, clasped his hands together and said, "Pretty good. I was a bit nervous, but I did what you suggested—saying hello and good-bye and making better eye contact. I was surprised that on the most part everyone responded positively and by the end of the work week I felt more relaxed."

"Excellent." I said. "I'm glad it worked out for you."

"Thanks," Tyler looked up and smiled, a smile that suggested that he was surprised that a simple basic suggestion—extensively in the realm of manners—would change his work experience so quickly.

Now that Tyler had some success in the social realm, I thought it might be an opportune time to help him go inward by offering him some tips on how to lower his day-to-day level of anxiety and hopefully eventually eliminate it.

"To build on last week's success, I'd like you to take a look at this sheet."

The sheet had a list of 14 different ways in which a person could manage anxiety and stress and prevent panic (Cohen-Posey, 2016).

"I'm game for anything," Tyler replied.

The sheet was divided into two columns. The left column had the anxiety reducing method and the right column described the changes those methods produced in the brain. Virtually all the anxiety and stress reducing methods sought to accomplish the same thing: Transition a person from the sympathetic nervous system to the parasympathetic, from a state of anxiety (fear) to a state of calm, (safety).

Tyler chose three. Cold to the forehead, sucking on peppermint Altoids, and thinking deliberately, counting backwards by threes from 100.

"You don't have to press the bottle of water against your forehead if you don't want to." I placed my fingers around a small bottle of Poland Spring without palming it. "The cold needs to be applied to the surface of your skin to stimulate the part of your brain that puts you in a calm state. The Altoids have the same effect on the brain. The counting is slightly different in that deliberate thinking transitions you to the cerebral cortex. But it's all good."

"I wish I knew this in high school," Tyler quipped.

"Me too," I replied. We both had a laugh.

"By the way. What was high school like for you?" I asked.

"Pretty miserable. My parents made me take advanced classes and play the double bass. I did well academically but hated it."

"Do you still play?"

"I haven't touched it since high school."

"How about socially?"

"It was pretty rough, especially when we were more independent, and our parents weren't running things. When I stopped BMX racing after middle school it seemed as if all my friends went their separate ways. High school was pretty lonely."

Based on the developmental history I recorded when Tyler was nine years old, he appeared to have overcome some of the emotional and social difficulties he was grappling with back then. Competing in Bicycle Motorcross (BMX) racing requires overcoming one's fears, cooperating with others, and being able to tolerate demographic transitions brought on by the extensive travel often required to compete within and outside your home state. Hypersensitive children have difficulty with all these challenges.

But I sensed that Tyler felt unduly pressured by his well-meaning parents from an early age to make and maintain a circle of friends, to do exceptionally well academically, to play a musical instrument throughout his school years. Additionally, they expected him to attend a highly regarded college of engineering far away from home against his wishes. But it was way too premature to encourage Tyler to address his relationship with his parents, even though he had recently prevailed in his desire not to return to the school he had been attending for two years; his emotional muscles were simply not built up enough to meet that challenge at this time.

Speaking of Tyler's parents. After a few sessions his mother sent me this text: "He really likes you. He likes the direct practical advice. The other therapists sat back and waited for him to talk. Thank you!"

When I saw Tyler next, I said, "I just wanted to let you know that your mother texted me a few days ago."

"What did she say?"

"Essentially, that we were a good match."

"So far so good." Tyler concurred.

"I'm glad you think so. But what about communication with your mom going forward? Is that all right?"

Tyler paused in thought. "I'll let her know that I can take it from here."

I am very flexible when he comes to communication with parents, even when I'm working with a young adult. It all depends on what we agree on from the start, and it's always subject to change.

A couple sessions later, Tyler came in smiling and said. "Something really funny happened at work. I hung around after work for the first time—I kind of like this girl that works my shift and I think she likes me—"

"Did something happen to make you feel that way?"

"She brushed up against my arm a couple times when we passed each other in the food set-up area." Tyler had a wiry physique but had muscular arms.

"But what happened that was funny?"

"I was involved—just a little—in the group conversation and she looked at me and said, "You're really human," and we all cracked up. "I didn't take it the wrong way, partly because she had a sparkle in her eye when she said it. She might have had a few beers too."

"Wow." I was actually dumb founded but tried not to let on.

"But there's even more. I just got a text inviting me to go out with her and some friends."

"After work?"

"No. This weekend."

"Nice," I replied.

Although I suspected that Tyler had little or no experience dating, I chose not to ask him to give me an accounting of his lack of sexual experience—even if that information might help me provide him with some guidance. It was too risky an avenue of inquiry this early in his therapy; for a near 20-year-old male to admit to having very limited experience sexually might be an embarrassing, even an emasculating exposure. Also, I have learned in my many decades as a therapist that in regard to sex, when a young man or woman becomes comfortable with dating, the rest will follow.

"Would you like some more communication tips?" I asked.

"Please."

I removed a few index cards from my desk that had conversation starters written on them. But first I wanted to provide Tyler with a guiding concept or two.

"O.K. Quick question. Do you know what people like to hear the sound of most?"

Tyler seemed to give it some thought. "Music?"

I shook my head. "The sound of their own voice."

"You got it." Tyler laughed. "You should meet my father. He can't stop talking." Tyler's father had a 40-year career in public relations. They were quite the match: a father that talks too much, a son that talks too little.

I proceeded to introduce the concept of reflective or active listening.

"According to Wikipedia Reflective listening 'is a communication strategy involving two key steps," I was now reading from one of the index cards. "The first step is seeking to understand a speaker's idea, then offering the idea back to the speaker, to confirm that the idea has been understood correctly."

Tyler nodded.

"But it doesn't have to be an idea per se; someone can simply be referring to the weather or a great baseball game or a movie they recently saw. Let's try a few examples."

"I went to the Yankee game last night." Tyler said.

"You went to the Yankee game?"

"Yeah. It was great."

"What was so great?" Framing the sentence as a question, as opposed to making a declarative statement, communicates to the speaker that you want to hear more.

"Sanchez hit a towering home run and Hicks made an unbelievable catch."

"How are Sanchez and Hicks doing overall this year? I know that they're been injured."

"Amazing when they're on the field."

"You're quite the Yankees fan!" I exclaimed.

"Since I was five. My whole family is." Tyler was smiling from ear to ear. I did not reveal to Tyler that I had been an avid Yankees fan for over 55 years. I wanted to remain his psychotherapist, not become his buddy.

I paused briefly. "So how did that feel?"

"How did what feel?"

"Our exchange?"

"Great!" The endorphins were now flowing.

We role played some more and then I provided him with a few conversation starters. "What would you do if given $2000.00 a week for life to live on?"

Follow up question one: "How would you use the money?"

Follow up question two: "Would this change your future plans?"

These questions usually generate a great deal of animated discussion among young adults possibly due to the fantastical nature of it and their concerns about the future.

"Do you have that on an index card?" Tyler laughed.

I handed him the card.

A few sessions later Tyler came in and said, "I'm in a pretty sticky situation at work. You know that girl I told you about?"

I nodded.

"We went out twice in a group and she wants to take it further and I really don't want to."

"Yeah. Things can get a little sticky dating people at work. But you have a right to choose whomever you want to date." My response was purposefully forceful and unequivocal. I wanted to make it abundantly clear that I didn't believe that Tyler was in some way desperate for experience—that he had to go out with any young woman that was willing—and even more important, I did not even want to risk the appearance of being another of those well-meaning adults who put undue pressure on him to do what they perceived to be in his interest, but not what he desired.

After returning from a two-week summer ending vacation, Tyler and I discussed the fall schedule.

"I'm feeling really good," he began. "And with school starting, I was wondering if I could come every two weeks?"

Usually, the winding down of therapy session frequency occurs toward the end of treatment. But in Tyler's case I responded affirmatively.

"As long as you're feeling better and have achieved some of the goals, we set down two months ago, why not?"

"I'm even doing deliveries at work. I make the same hourly wage as I did taking orders but now I'm loading up on tips."

"Hellos, good-byes and good friendly eye-contact pays off in more ways than one."

24

After our next session, Tyler gave his parents' permission to come in and see me.

When Tyler's parents walked into my office, our encounter, unlike the last time I saw them ten years previous, was all smiles and handshakes and great to "see you" again. After an exchange of pleasantries, Tyler's mother, Ann, quipped excitedly, "Did you hear?"

"Hear what?"

"Tyler has a girlfriend!"

"Nice. Anyone from work?"

"No. The gym. She's perfect for him. She's a high school senior. The other girl was moving too fast for him."

I was about to reply "Well, when you look like James Dean..." but I didn't.

"It's so cute," Ann continued. "He picks her up from school every day."

"Wow. Have you met her?"

"Yes. She's eaten over a few times."

I turned to Tyler's father Jack, "What do you make of all of this."

"What a difference a couple of months make." Jack tapped his knuckles on the wooden side table.

We went on to discuss the family's communication difficulties, particularly Tyler's unwillingness to respond at any length to his father's entreaties regarding his work and school life for fear that he will be given unsolicited advice or be judged or even criticized.

"Although he's come such a long way socially, he still rarely says a word to me. We can't even talk about the weather."

Since Jack didn't directly acknowledge his part in the disconnect from his son, I chose not to pursue the issue to avoid alienating him.

"You're quite different in this way," I said sympathetically.

"We sure are." Jack replied.

"Would you like to try to make some improvements in this area?"

"We can give it a try."

I extended my hand in Jack's direction. He shook it firmly.

"We'll give it a try." I said.

Tyler's communication difficulties, particularly with his father, were long-standing. Hypersensitive children or more clinically stated, children with sensory integration over-sensitivity, are typically speakers of too few or too many words (Healy, 2011). Both communication postures are defensive, keeping incoming stimuli at bay. Unfortunately, this is often misinterpreted by others—parents, peers and teachers alike—as oppositional in nature, when it is an attempt to solve a (exteroceptive) neurological problem: How do I manage incoming stimuli when everything seems too much and feels so intense? Well-meaning moms and dads too often feel it is their duty to force their hypersensitive child to engage the world in age-appropriate and timely manner. I often counsel a form of strategic accommodation, depending on the degree of hypersensitivity the child exhibits.

Tyler's father Jack was engaging and verbose and often was frustrated by Tyler's long verbal pauses and silences and reluctance to do anything with him. Although Tyler's mother Ann was more understanding of his sensitivities and social anxiety, she still insisted on his participating in BMX racing and orchestra through his middle and high school years. Even though Tyler disliked these activities and resented his parents for forcing him to participate in them, these types of semi-structured activities may have helped Tyler develop the capacity to interact more comfortably with others and modify his sensitivities, albeit at the expense of his relationship with his parents.

But forcing Tyler to go to a college he hated from the moment he stepped on campus and continuing to surveil his grades as if he were still in primary school, drove Tyler further from his father's (and mother's) orbit.

"I don't talk to him," Tyler confessed. "Because I think he's going to judge everything I do."

"Still?" I inquired.

"Still." Tyler's reply was firm.

I paused momentarily, then said. "Let's review."

"Ok."

"Just these last three months you were able to accomplish some important goals regarding your independence from your father. You were able to transfer from a faraway engineering college to a local liberal arts school against your father's wishes and you nipped in the bud his short-lived attempt at over seeing your current test scores. You worked hard at the pizzeria—scaling a wall of anxiety in the process—to save enough money to buy the car you wanted, without your father's assistance or interference. You've done a terrific job."

"Thanks." Tyler was misty-eyed.

I titled my head to the right slightly and lifted my eyes toward Tyler's face.

"Things have changed, right?"

"Right." Tyler said.

"On both sides," I continued. Tyler nodded.

"Yes. They have."

Although Tyler appeared to have little interest in bridging the gap between him and his father—at home or through therapy—I thought that it was important to state the obvious: that the dynamic between he and his father and mother had changed and that there was a closer relationship with them in the offering if he so desired and on more equitable terms.

During the next few months, I saw less and less of Tyler. During the Christmas break from school, I met with him and his father together for a second time and it was still a terribly awkward coupling. I sensed that they were uncomfortable even sitting near each other in my office. I too was uncomfortable, unable to find an appropriate time—a clear therapeutic space—to air the grievances that they had privately shared with me and for years had harbored toward each other.

My intuition told me that Tyler was happy with his new life, channelling his energies toward a new form of study and that special high school senior that made his heart bloom. Similarly, his dad, recently retired, was beginning to enjoy his new-born freedom, going skiing and fishing with old friends and taking road trips to reconnect with cousins he had grown up with in Colorado. Perhaps, with the passing of time and maturity, Tyler and his father would find a comfortable place to communicate in the future.

References

Amlie, J. (2018). The Parasympathetic Nervous System: Helplessness/Freeze. *Blue Earth Awakening*, retrieved from: https://www. blueearthawakening.com/trauma--the- nervous-system.html

Arky, B. (2018). Treating sensory processing issues. *Child Mind Institute*. Retrieved from: https://childmind.org/article/treating-sensory-processing-issues/

Cohen-Posey, K. (2016). Neuroscience for Clinicians. Video program. Retrieved from: https://catalog.pesi.com/item/neuro- science-clinicians-brain-change-anxiety-trauma-impulse-control-depres- sion-relationships-13594

Dahlitz, M. (2017). *The Psychotherapists Essential Guide to The Brain*. Park Ridge, Australia: Dahlitz Media.

Healy, M. (2011). The Highly Sensitive Child, Maureen Healy. *Psychology Today*, retrieved from: https://www.psychologytoday.com/ au/ blog/creative-development/201106/ the-highly-sensitive-child

Four-year-old Domingo Resolves Trauma Through Art

"Whoof! Whoof!" the compact size boy leaped forward, his small hands jutting out like paws, striking down at the carpeted floor. "Whoof! Whoof!"

I had been working at the Head Start Center for two years as a disability consultant. Although I was a pediatric clinical social worker by profession, the school's director had taught me how to administer a preschool screening test to evaluate whether or not a child had a learning, emotional or physical disability. If a child did turn out to have a special need, I arranged for and oversaw services provided by various helping professionals: visiting special education teachers; speech pathologists; occupational and physical therapists. If the child was suffering from an emotional disturbance, I was the one who provided the play therapy.

Upon return from a two-week Christmas break, a teacher from the program pulled me aside in the hallway outside her classroom. "Can you help us with a child? He's barking like a dog and jumping around the room and scaring other children. We don't know what to do."

"Yes. I'll come by to observe him soon."

Shortly thereafter, I met The Boy Who Needed to Act Like A Dog.

Domingo was barely four years old. One night, it was reported, he woke up in a daze, walked into the living room, opened up the cage where the family's dog presumably spent the night. The dog was apparently agitated enough to take a bite out of Domingo's face. When Domingo returned to school after the break, he had a thick bandage across his left cheek. Domingo told his teacher that the dog bit him. The school reported the incident to Child Protective Services and a case worker immediately visited the school, photographed Domingo's face, then visited his home.

I sat in the back of the classroom and casually observed Domingo. During circle time he participated in song intermittently but needed to be prompted and guided when the children transitioned from one play activity to another. At lunch he ate slowly, almost absent-mindedly, as if he were preoccupied, in a trance.

"Can I see his file?" I asked the school's director.

Domingo's profile rendered a picture of a child who up until recently had been developing nicely, meeting all developmental milestones. He liked playing with blocks and Legos and was able to draw with "**unusual accuracy**" for a four-year-old boy.

I contacted the CPS case worker and he arranged for me to visit Domingo's house. The CPS worker told me: "Apparently the dog's a beloved family pet and has never exhibited any aggression toward adults or children or other dogs. Their neighbors confirmed this. This family isn't going to give up this dog without a fight. We decided that if we got a court order to remove the dog, even temporarily, the family might take flight. That might put the boy further at risk. People are really crazy about their dogs. They sometimes treat them better than their kids."

The irony of what the case worker last said wasn't lost upon me.

Domingo lived with his family on the far Eastern end of the County. His wood-framed house stood on what seemed like stilts, hoisting its skeletal structure about six feet above ground. The house abutted a river from which its overflow tended to flood the area during storms and mighty nor'easters.

I climbed the wooden stairs and knocked on the door. Domingo's father greeted me cordially. "Come in," he said.

The floorboards of the house were worn but looked as though they had recently been scrubbed and swept clean. There was an old fashion wood burning stove to the rear of the living room and the dog, a Rottweiler, appeared to be asleep, face down on a white woolen pad, in its cage.

Domingo's father led me through the living room and into a linoleum tiled kitchen. "Coffee?" he asked.

"Yes, thank you."

Domingo's family had been living in the area since the 1950's and owned their home free and clear, he proudly stated. His father, grandfather and uncles were all fishermen; his mother was a school lunch lady. I asked Domingo's father about his son's present functioning.

"He eats well, goes to the bathroom on his own and sleeps through the night."

"No nightmares?" I asked.

Domingo's father shook his head. "None."

"Very good." I smiled.

"What about friends? Does he play with other children?"

"Domingo gets along with everyone. He has lots of cousins. We're all very close." Domingo's father pointed toward pictures on the wall.

"Terrific."

We talked about Domingo's behavior in the classroom and about the school's concerns. Interestingly, he didn't bark or jump around like a dog in his home.

"I know that they're looking out for his welfare," Domingo's father said.

"And I am too."

Before leaving, I reassured Domingo's father that I had not come to his home to try and have his dog taken away, but to introduce myself and get his permission to evaluate and possibly work with his son if needed.

"When my wife gets home, I'll show her the permission slips. We'll get back to you by the end of the week."

"Thanks for the coffee." I shook Domingo's father's extended hand.

As a young therapist, I learned the hard way, about being too assertive with parents who may or may not have intentionally done harm to their children. I would let my emotions get in the way. In Domingo's case, I had to bond with his parents through focusing on the Domingo emotional needs, not the dog or their possible role in Domingo getting bit. The CPS worker involved in the case knew this as well. If the dog was removed from the home by court decree, the family might take off and Domingo would be without any support at all and would be forever blamed for telling his teachers that he had been bitten by the family dog. If the dog was removed and the family stayed in the area, they would surely blame the school for the removal of a beloved family pet and likely disenroll Domingo from the school and possibly subject him to family shaming, compounding his traumatic injury. Furthermore, if the dog was as well behaved as reported by the family, Domingo and their neighbors, an injustice would have been committed by hastily removing the dog and possibly having him destroyed. If Domingo was to suddenly lose his school, his loving teachers, his classmates and his therapist, his life would be altered forever. The stakes were very high. I had to proceed with the warmth of an objective but caring scientist.

The very next day, Domingo's father dropped off the permission slips at the school. I took my position in the rear of the classroom and quietly observed Domingo, taking notes from time to time. I noticed that when he played by himself with blocks or a garage set, he appeared focused and in the moment. But when other children crossed his path, his body tensed up defensively. Then, suddenly it happened.

"Whoof! Whoof!" Domingo leaped forward, more like a frog than a dog. "Whoof! Whoof!"

The children around him froze and one began to cry. The assistant teacher gently led the frightened children away. "It's ok," the teacher whispered. "Domingo's just play acting."

The head teacher positioned herself on the floor a few feet away from Domingo. "Are you ok?" she inquired, sympathetically.

Domingo seemed to stare right through her. "Domingo. Are you all right, honey?"

Domingo nodded. The teacher stayed near him for a while, then asked. "Would you like to color?"

Domingo nodded. The teacher moved closer to Domingo, took his hand, stood up and walked him over to a table near her desk at the front of the room.

The teacher motioned over to another child, "Sammy. Come and color with me and Domingo."

This teacher somehow instinctively knew that what Domingo needed most was a connection to a caring adult, not admonishment, or isolation from other children.

I was deeply moved by the gentle and caring ways in which the teachers responded to Domingo, while at the same time attending to the children who found themselves within the frightening sphere of Domingo's distress. When a child, or for that matter an adult, repeats something over and over again, in Domingo's case, the barking and acting like a dog, the repetition usually represents an attempt to resolve a psychic conflict or discharge pent up traumatic energy. Was Domingo attempting to do both?

That afternoon I met with the school's director, Domingo's teacher, the classroom assistants and the school's consulting psychologist to develop a plan to manage Domingo in the classroom and also to create conditions for him to resolve any internal conflicts that resulted from his distressing encounter with the family dog. Domingo apparently needed to unburden himself of the psychic energy that was still bound up inside him, and as a team, we would try to help discharge it.

"I think what you and the assistant teachers are doing is incredible, " I told them. "When Domingo has his outbursts, stay calm, stay sympathetic. If the other children are upset, continue to reassure them; comfort the ones who are upset. Try to keep Domingo in the classroom, casually moving him through the day with assistance."

"Do you think that you can work with him individually? He could use some therapy," the director said.

"I agree, and I have an idea. I think I know how to help him."

"Great."

"I'm going to try to use his drawing ability to defuse some of that bound up energy. But let me start with him in the classroom."

My working hypothesis regarding Domingo's internal conflict was that there might be a discrepancy between what actually happened in his encounter with the dog and what he was told by his parents and what his parents subsequently told the school and Child Protective Services. The dog was most likely non-aggressive, as described by Domingo's father and confirmed by his neighbors. But how the dog bit Domingo didn't make complete sense to me. In the time it would have taken Domingo to approach the cage, open the latch and swing the door open, the dog would have had ample time to awake from his slumber, reorient himself and recognize Domingo as non-threatening, and wouldn't have been startled into attack mode. I believed that the story that Domingo's parents were telling all concerned was half-concoction—half truth, made up to protect the dog and save him from the pound. A more likely scenario was that the dog was already out of the cage and both he and Domingo, in the dead of night, neither one fully awake, somehow converged, *made contact*, and the dog spontaneously lashed out. Even though Domingo didn't have a fully conscious recollection of what occurred—most people don't recall life-threatening confrontations--he probably had an implicit, *an unconscious*, memory of what happened and his barking and leaping like dog was an expression of it, a symptom of post-traumatic stress. Thus, Domingo's seemingly herculean challenge was to somehow unburden himself of this conflict without betraying his parents and the beloved family dog.

Treating trauma and the symptoms of post-traumatic stress is difficult in any case, but with children it takes a therapist into unknown territory; you're mostly *feeling* your way through. The cognitive work, the psychoeducation that an adult would initially receive and then, later on, instructions on how to reduce the intensity of their symptoms (before deeper, more intense therapeutic interventions can be considered), are not amenable to the treatment of very young children because they are developmentally unable to conceptualize.

The next day I drafted an outline of how I would approach my treatment of Domingo in the classroom and gave a copy to each staff member so that they would know what I was doing at all times, know when to assist me and when to keep their distance.

I motioned to one of the assistant teachers, Miss Mary, to sit with me near Domingo on the classroom floor and initiate play between us. Although he was already familiar with my presence, I didn't want to risk frightening him or even making him uncomfortable by sitting next to him before being formally introduced.

"Let's build a house," Miss Mary said to Domingo, pointing to a clear bin of large Lego pieces. "Mr. Roger is going help us." Miss Mary's choice of Legos was right on the mark. Domingo had already demonstrated a mastery of Lego building and this increased the chances of our initial encounter being a success.

The three of us took turns stacking the Lego pieces one on top of the other as a towering structure of red and yellow bricks began to rise. "Muy bien," I said, uttering two of the dozen or so words I knew in Spanish. "You're a very good builder, Domingo."

Domingo smiled, causing the raw reddish scar that lined the left side of his face to stretch and glow.

"What color is this Lego piece?" I asked.

"Red," he answered.

"Excellent."

"How about this one?"

"Yellow."

"Boy, do you know your colors. Doesn't he, Miss Mary?" That was her cue to take leave.

"Domingo. I'm going to help Miss Nancy with the lunches. Have fun building with Mr. Roger."

We played with the Lego bricks for a few more minutes, running a car up and over the side and roof of the house, laughing at our silliness all the while.

"That was a lot of fun," I said to Domingo. "But it smells like lunch time. "I'll see you tomorrow."

The next day Miss Mary called Domingo over to the classroom drawing table and I joined them. After some free form parallel drawing, I took out a few thick white pieces of paper upon which there where letters and shapes in black bold print. I placed one on the table. "Can you copy the letter A?" I asked Domingo.

Domingo nodded, confidently. With a firm steady hand, he copied the letter A almost precisely as it had been printed.

"Excellent." I said. I placed another sheet of paper on the table. "Can you copy the circle?"

Smiling, without saying a word, Domingo copied the circle as precisely as he had the letter A.

I was getting excited.

With a firm, steady confident hand, Domingo continued to demonstrate an uncanny ability to replicate the letters and shapes that I set before him. I had only known one other child that was able to do this at such a young age and she grew up to be a prominent illustrator for Walt Disney Productions without the benefit of formal training.

The next time I saw Domingo, I asked him to join me at the Play-Doh and hard clay table and help me mold animals and people. "I'll need to use the Play-Doh tools," I said to him. "I'm probably not nearly as good at this as you are."

I began to soften up a mound of hard clay for Domingo and asked. "Can you make a boy out of this?"

Domingo proceeded to flatten a portion of the clay to create what seemed like the base of a body, added a head, then arms and legs. He took a pencil and carefully sculpted a recognizable face, then fingers and toes. I was stunned. It was as if the godhead had arisen from Domingo's little hands.

"Wow, Domingo. You really know how to draw and mold clay!"

I continued to see Domingo in the classroom over the next few weeks, cultivating a relationship with him through play. Although his outbursts were fewer and less intense and in duration, I only partly attributed this to his therapy, but more so to the passing of time. The healing of the gash on his face and the forming of a protective scar were quite helpful to him. Also, equally important, the tension in his home had recently been defused, as a result of his parents not being found to have been neglectful of Domingo's welfare by CPS. Their beloved dog was safe; he would not be removed.

Since his symptoms appeared to be diminishing and the risk of retraumatizing him reduced, I decided to introduce him to pictures of people and animals, images that might trigger some of the traumatic energy still bound up inside of him. We took turns drawing the pictures with pencils, crayons and magic markers, but I purposely didn't present him with a picture of a dog.

Domingo's reproductions of these more challenging images took more of his time and weren't nearly as precise as his replications of shapes and letters: however, his deliberateness, his apparent *strategizing*, as he approached the rendering of the images before him, were even more impressive indications of the artist's brain at work.

At about week five, after at least 10 sessions, I told the school staff that they had created a very safe environment for Domingo and helped me carve out a therapeutic space for us to work in, so I wouldn't have to take him out of the classroom. "I think he's doing much better. What is your impression?"

"He's doing much, much better, " the head teacher stated. "He barks much less and seems much calmer, more like the child that came to us before the biting incident. The children are no longer afraid of him."

"It really helps when he's no longer leaping around the room," I jokingly pointed out.

"It sure does," the director blurted out, laughing.

I explained to the group that with their help and guidance I was able to establish a trusting and playful relationship with Domingo. Subsequently, I would soon be trying more direct interventions in an attempt to reduce and eventually drain the last of the traumatic energy still bound up inside of him. "I will be very careful, though. One small step at a time."

The term used to describe this stage in Domingo's therapy is titration. Titration is a term borrowed from the field of chemistry; it's a way of measuring changes in a given solution by adding small amounts of other substances and monitoring and recording the changes every step of the way. This is what high school students do in the lab as an extension of what they learned in the classroom.

The treatment of trauma with a client is similar to the one a chemist employs in the lab. Initially, it has four carefully timed steps: psychoeducation; analysis by the therapist of the distorted thinking arising from the traumatic event; the identification of triggers; and the reduction of symptoms associated with PTS through biofeedback techniques. When these four objectives are accomplished, deeper work can commence, without too high a risk of retraumatizing the client through over exposure to the traumatic memory.

My sessions with Domingo utilizing art laid the groundwork for me to initiate the titration process by encouraging him to do a pictorial rendering— the drawing of pictures—of the biting incident with his dog or anything related to his implicit or even his explicit memory of the experience. I could only employ this therapeutic modality with a child as young as Domingo because of his extraordinarily precocious artistic ability. But first I would have to test the emotional waters for levels of turbulence.

I started the next session with Domingo by presenting him with pictures of family pets: cats, birds, dogs and rabbits.

"I have two birds and a cat," I said. "Do you have any of these pets in your home?"

Domingo pointed at a dog.

"You have a dog? What's his name?"

"Sammy."

"Sammy?"

Domingo nodded.

"What does Sammy do all day?"

"He sleeps," Domingo started to giggle.

"Does he ever get up to eat?"

Domingo nodded his head up and down, laughing all the while.

"Is Sammy like Daisy The Lazy Dog?" I showed Domingo the cover of a book that the teacher had read to the class a few days before.

"Yes!" Domingo was now delirious with laughter. "But he's a boy!"

"Right. Sammy's a boy dog—who sleeps and eats all day. What was I thinking?" I tapped my head lightly and shook it from side to side, feigning disbelief over what I had said.

The introduction of pets that reside in homes--dogs in general and then Domingo's dog Sammy in particular, allowed the safe triggering—the loosening up--of some of the traumatic energy bound up inside of him. This came about principally because he was able to creatively and playfully engage the subject matter without being overwhelmed by the underlying implicit, *unconscious,* memory of being bitten. This was also made possible by working with a therapist, who's only vested interest was *his* welfare, not the protection of the family dog.

Subsequently, instead of erupting, barking and leaping around like a dog, *impulsively expressing the traumatic energy bound up inside him*, Domingo was able to accomplish a controlled and proportional release of this energy through play and through his art, diminishing its potency and strange hold over him.

Domingo's laughter gradually died down, but before I asked him to help me put the pictures and the book away, I extended my hand to him and said, "You sure know your dogs."

Domingo shook my hand and suddenly, almost shyly, turned away.

By the following week Domingo's barking in the classroom was barely a whisper—his body movements more of a crawl then a leap. There was nothing menacing or frightening about his utterances or body movements and the other children just went along with it until it past. Subsequently, I reduced our weekly sessions from two to one time a week.

Before our next session, I called Domingo's father and asked if he could send Domingo into school with a picture of his family with Sammy the dog in it.

When I received it from Domingo's teacher, I glued it to the middle of a thick sheet of white paper.

"Thanks for bringing in the picture," I said to Domingo. "Who is this?"

"Mommy."

"Who is this?"

"Poppy."

"Who is this?

"Me." Domingo laughed.

"That's you?"

"Yes."

"You've grown so big." I gradually widened my hands.

Domingo continued to smile.

"And who's this? Daisy the Lazy Dog?"

"No! That's Sammy!"

"That's right," I said. "That's your dog Sammy."

I took out a piece of paper and started to draw Domingo's family from the photo. "I'm having a hard time with this. Can you help me with this drawing of your family?"

Domingo nodded. I gave him a few pieces of wider sheets of paper, so he had enough room to draw all the figures side by side if he so desired. He drew his mother, father, himself and Sammy the dog in that order. His mother was roundish, his father tall and thin, himself small and round and the dog long and bulky. All the figures received dotted eyes, noses and lips like his clay moldings.

"Excellent." I said.

Domingo smiled.

I set his drawing of his family members and the photo of his family side by side and asked.

"In the picture of your mommy is she happy or sad?"

"Happy."

"How about Poppy? Happy or sad?"

"Happy."

"How about Domingo? Happy or sad?"

"Happy."

"Don't forget Sammy the dog? Happy or sad?"

"Happy." Domingo replied.

Domingo's replies were calm and quiet.

"So," I said as a way of summing up our session, "Your mom and dad and you and Sammy the dog are happy."

Domingo nodded affirmatively, without saying a word.

A few days later, with the assistance of Miss Mary, Domingo presented the photo and his drawing of his family to his classmates during show and tell. Domingo told them about the time they all went fishing together on his father's boat and Sammy the Dog slept the whole way through.

Since Domingo was doing so well, I decided not to address—or have him address—the memory of the biting incident. Instead, the Head Start center consulted with an art teacher and set up an enrichment program for him in the classroom. I continued to see him every other week until the spring semester came to an end and the school turned into a three-days per week summer camp in which the children were taken on day trips to places like Sesame Street Park, petting zoos and indoor aquariums.

In the fall, upon returning from summer break, I was told by the director that Domingo had transitioned successfully to a preschool/kindergarten program in his school district that promised to cultivate his artistic ability. With his parent's permission, I sent copies of Domingo's artwork to his new teachers. A few months later, I contacted Domingo's father and his new preschool teacher and they both assured me that he was doing well.

Further Reading:

The Emotional Backpack: Managing Conflict Resolution with Children of Trauma, Carly Ly, LMSW, Active Learner, Fall 2018.

Dibs: In Search of Self: personality development in play therapy, Virginia Axline, Houghton Mifflin, 1964.

The 10 Core Competencies For Evidence-Based Treatment, Trauma, PTSD, Grief & Loss, Mike Dubi, ED.D, LMHC, LPS, NCC, Patrick Powell, ED.D, LMHC, LPC, NCC, J. Eric Gentry, PhD, LMHC, PESI Publishing & Media, 2019.

Daisy The Lazy Dog, K. Young. The ABC Silly Animal Series Book I, 2016.

How to Implement Trauma-informed Care to Build Resilience to Childhood Trauma, Jessica Dym Bartlett, Kate Steber, Child Trends, May 9, 2019,

Somatic Attachment & Trauma Resolution, Hazel Williams-Carter, CH RRT, www.HealingTraumaCenter.com, 2020.

Play Therapy with Traumatized Children – A Prescriptive Approach, Paris Goodyear-Brown, Wiley, 2009.

THROUGH ILLNESS A VETERAN FACES AND OVERCOMES HIS PAINFUL PAST

I met John in September of 1982, a mere four months into my first job as a clinical social worker. I had been hired by a mental health center primarily to work with children and adolescents. But due to the recession, there was a high demand for affordable mental health services, thus I was scheduled to see adults as well.

John was a 34-year-old U.S. Navy Veteran, Vietnam War era. A "radio man" on a ship that patrolled the world's major waterways, John was well travelled by the time his three-year enlistment ended in 1969. If my memory serves me correctly, he came to sessions wearing a green army jacket, a Star of Christopher dangling, intermittently, from his neck. One thing I knew for sure though, John was in great distress.

"This anxiety is killing me," he said, struggling to hold back tears. "And no one seems to be able to help."

John had seen a psychiatrist in a private practice a few times, but the medicine he prescribed—an anti-anxiety medication—wasn't helping and he couldn't afford to continue to pay the high private fees.

"Hopefully, our psychiatrist, Dr. W., can help." I replied.

Since I was an unattached, under-employed therapist—I was still parking cars in Manhattan on weekends—I not only had enough free time to see John three times a week but also was able to speak to him by telephone between sessions.

Despite my efforts and the medicine that Dr. W. had prescribed him—a different anti-anxiety medication —John continued to get worse.

"I'm having a terrible time getting out of the house."

41

Due to my inexperience, I was unclear of what was causing John's distress. From a textbook point of view though, I was beginning to suspect that he was in the throes of an agoraphobic breakdown, given his nearly paralyzing level of anxiety, particularly when faced with what had become the daunting task of leaving his house.

Eventually, John turned to the Veterans Hospital for help. It turned out that he had been misdiagnosed. Although John presented with intense, persistent and overwhelming feelings of anxiety, his history indicated that he was suffering from a form of low-grade, chronic depression, dysthymia (John Hopkins, n.d.), the anxiety a symptom of it. According to his new psychiatrist, Dr. Campanella, John was able to cope with his dysthymia most of his life through adaptive and maladaptive behaviors; however, due to a series of losses over the years and a TIA, a transient ischemic attack (Mayo Clinic, n.d.), in May, those long standing, mostly successful, methods of coping became increasingly ineffective.

Dr. Campanella described John's anxiety as a leak in his biochemical system. "John's coping behaviors acted as caulking and due to his accumulated losses, the caulking popped. I'm hoping that the medication I prescribed will refill the holes and stop the leak."

Dr. Campanella prescribed John the anti-depressant, Elavil. During a six-week period, John's anxiety gradually dissipated, and he was able to return to work.

"It wasn't just the medicine that helped," John asserted. "It was the puzzle too."

As a young therapist, not necessarily knowing how to help John through the first weeks of his crisis, I recommended that he go to the local Five & Dime, and purchase the largest jigsaw puzzle he could find. My intuition was that the puzzle could serve to focus John's attention and occupy his time while he was home from work. John's self-esteem had been badly bruised as a result of not being able to work and support his family in the way he had become accustomed. I instructed him to set it up on his dining room table and begin to work at it as soon as he got up in the morning, to avoid falling into a pattern of negative thinking.

"My father left when I was five and it was hard growing up. I vowed never to be like him."

"We'll have lots of time to talk about your dad, but for now let's concentrate on getting you feeling better. Work that puzzle, every tiny piece, until it's done." I suddenly sounded like the headmaster of a private school I attended as a teenager.

It would be decades before the word ruminate—and the belief that ruminating promoted ill mental health—would enter my vocabulary and become an important addition to my conceptual framework. But ruminating was exactly what John had been doing. I felt that if John's focus could be directed away from negative thoughts, he could assist in his own recovery more effectively, while the medicine, Elavil, hopefully worked its wonders. A 10,000-piece jigsaw puzzle was user-friendly and challenging at the same time. Most importantly, it was at the ready to use when negative thoughts entered John's mind and threatened to dominate his waking hours and undermine his treatment.

While concentrating on providing immediate relief for John, I had not attended to John's feelings of abandonment. Why hadn't I encouraged him to further explore his feelings about his father leaving the family when he was five years old?

Once again, I was a young, inexperienced therapist, thrust into the life of a navy veteran whose life was possibly on the verge of collapse, without a safe harbor in sight. Since I had little to no experience working with adults, I could only draw upon the research I had recently done for my master's thesis on compulsive gambling and Gambler's Anonymous. I concluded that an individual in recovery from an addiction needed to be abstinent, "clean," for several years before starting a traditional form of psychotherapy. Exploring painful childhood experiences could be emotionally destabilizing and make an individual in early recovery vulnerable to relapse. I applied the same logic to John, but with a shorter time frame as a guide. I believed that John needed a period of emotional stability before he could begin to explore his painful and possibly traumatic past, lest he risk upending the progress he was beginning to make.

During the next six months, John's anxiety all but vanished and his mood improved significantly. Subsequently, he reduced his therapy sessions from three a week, to two, to one. Nonetheless, John still hungered to give shape and order to his painful past, endeavoring to understand himself more deeply, more clearly.

"My father has always been a central figure in my life, even though I haven't seen him in 30 years." John's father had died in 1967.

"How come?" I asked.

"Well, even though my mother's mother and father took me and my sisters in with open arms, they were enraged at my father for leaving us. Every time I did something wrong, my grandmother would say, "You're just like your father.""

"Ouch."

"Ouch is right!"

Unfortunately, John grew up fearing that any wrong move he made could result in his being compared to his father, a man that was looked upon with distain by his mother's entire family.

"How did you cope?" I asked.

John chuckled sarcastically. "I made sure that I did what I was told. I did well in school. I never got in trouble."

John was an excellent student and was able to gain entry to one of New York City's elite high schools, by achieving high scores in math and science.

"How come you didn't go to college?" (Many graduates of New York City's elite high schools received scholarships to the country's most prestigious schools.)

"That wasn't our way. We were working class and very patriotic. So, as soon as I graduated high school, I enlisted in the Navy. I didn't see any combat, but a whole lot of ocean. And we were always at the ready."

After being discharged from the Navy, John resumed his relationship with his childhood sweetheart, Patricia, and they married a year later. Soon he was the father of two children, a boy and a girl, and moved from their city apartment to the suburbs. In 1975, he landed a job working for the NYC Department of Transportation, repairing buses and putting to use the mechanical and design skills he acquired in high school. For 30 years, except for that six-week hiatus in 1982, John rose from bed at 4:30 A.M. and took the 5:13 train into the city to start work at 7. Some nights he didn't get home until 11:00 P.M.

"Although I liked my job and the people I worked with, it was actually about that time that I began to feel something was wrong, emotionally."

John's eyes began to mist, as he looked away. "My grandmother died in 1975. My mother and grandfather in 1978. Also, a couple of older friends died too."

"That's a lot of loss to absorb in such a short time," I said.

John, now weeping, covered his face with his hands, his voice rising in misguided apology for expressing his grief. "Sorry," he said. "Sorry."

"Perhaps this flow of feeling is a long time coming."

John nodded in agreement, as his hands absorbed the tears that flooded his face.

Minutes later, John lifted his head and shook it from right to left, as if to reorient himself. "Wow."

Wow is right. It was becoming increasingly clear that John had been and still was suffering from unresolved grief. My working hypothesis was that his grief was neither simple nor complicated, but rather, unexpressed. But what were its origins? What were its entanglements? In other words, was the loss of his father and years later the loss of his maternal grandparents and mother all tangled up? One thing I knew for certain though, that the accumulative effect of these losses had been weighing heavily on John's psyche for a long time.

One of the extra benefits of working with John, was my collaboration with his psychiatrist, Dr. Campanella. I consulted with him about John's treatment every three months or so over the phone. He was a gentle, compassionate man who appeared to care deeply for John and was willing to speak with me at length about his progress. Over time, our discussions broadened beyond John's specific issues of grief, touching upon many other mental health subjects. Almost, seamlessly, Dr. Campanella became my first mentor in the field of mental health.

My talks with Dr. Campanella led to the conceptualization of two levels of human functioning based on his, our, understanding of the psyche, survival and compensation. From this perspective, John had been operating predominately from a compensatory position, with way too much of his characterological energy expended in the service of doing for and pleasing others. This kind of "compulsive caretaker" orientation, might have held John's implicit belief that he was no good, or never good enough, was "just like his old man," at bay. Yet left him vulnerable to falling into a lower level of functioning if his system took too many blows. His losses over the years and his TIA, did not appear to be traumatic but their combined accumulative effect was equally corrosive and ultimately led to significant stress response impairment, (Levine, 1976).

Individuals functioning predominately on a survival level, tend to have unstable lives. They're typically unable to hold down jobs for long and are often tobacco, drug or alcohol dependent. Furthermore, individuals operating in a survival mode, have relationships with others upon whom they are solely dependent, subjecting them to exploitation and abuse. In some cases, though, they find refuge in a relationship with a compulsive care giver. In the long run, though, this type of arrangement is susceptible to very poor mental health outcomes for the taker and giver as well.

I explained these concepts to John, and he quickly identified with compulsive giving. "I've always been Johnny on the spot. If anyone called, particularly when it came to automobile repair or electrical work, I was there. Even if I was in the middle of eating dinner. I'd go."

"Wow. Did you get paid for your work?"

"I never took a dime from anyone."

"Did they reciprocate in other ways?"

"Come to think of it, not anything I can remember."

"What about offering to baby-sit your kids? A card for your birthday? A pie for Thanksgiving?"

"No." John shook his head.

"There's nothing wrong with giving, but when it's extremely lopsided, when there's no obvious material benefit or some form of reciprocity, it's more like giving yourself away."

"No kidding," John replied.

John and I went on to explore his relationships with his family members, neighbors, friends and coworkers. He concluded that all the relationships had one thing in common: they were all imbalanced. John was the giver; they were the takers.

"But how do I say no? I've been doing this for so long."

"Well, since we're agreeing that your response is automatic, that you're behaving as if you don't have a choice in the matter, you need to develop stop gaps."

"What do you mean?"

"Well, what are your options when someone calls?"

"Not answer the phone?" John laughed.

"O.K.," I replied. "But that would be a freeze-like response. It wouldn't necessarily counter the compulsive nature of your response or alter the relationship with the person calling. But it would be better than nothing."

"Better than nothing is not what I'm here for," John was resolute.

"Good. Let's try some role-playing. Make believe you're a neighbor calling for help."

After a short pause John said, "John? This is Bob."

"Hi Bob," I replied invitingly. "How are you?"

"Good. How's it going on your end?

"We're all fine."

"Good. Very good. We've got an electrical problem over here. Can you come by and take a look?"

"I'm eating dinner right now. Can I call you back later?"

"O.k. But will you be able to come by?"

"I'm not sure. I'll call you later."

John was smiling sheepishly.

"On my part, playing you, what was the common theme?"

"You were non-committal."

"That's right. I purposely slowed down the process in order to think deliberately, not react compulsively."

"It's not going to be easy, especially with my relatives, but I'm going to follow through. I kind of think that my health is dependent on it."

"Kind of?" I said, somewhat sarcastically.

John and I laughed in unison at his attempt to soft-pedal the connection between his compulsive caregiving and the decline of his health.

Over the next few months, John's propensity to give "himself away" was tested several times.

"The nerve of them. They even called my wife to complain, to see if I was "all right."

"What did your wife tell them?"

"That I was slowing down, on doctor's orders."

"Excellent. Do you know what she was doing when she was saying that?"

"Well, she was protecting me for one thing. But essentially that things had changed, I changed, and this was the way it was going to be until further notice."

John even changed his approach to overtime at work. He respectfully declined or stayed over at a relative's house in Brooklyn when he worked into the night. Subsequently, he wouldn't have to endure the long train ride home and reverse it in the morning, after having gotten only a few hours of sleep.

"Congratulations!" I declared. "You're not only saying 'no' to impromptu or unreasonable requests, but you're asking for help?"

"What do you mean?"

"You asked a relative if you could stay overnight, when you did overtime."

"That's right. I never thought of it that way."

I thought this was an opportunity to further explore a subject we had discussed a few months earlier. "Remember a couple of months ago when we started talking about making behavioral changes?"

"Yes."

"Well, I wanted to see if I could lead you to a deeper understanding of the dynamics and thinking behind it."

"I'm all ears."

"Let's return to the concept of compulsive or automatic caring—the old 'Johnny on the spot.' The way I framed it initially was why would you have relationships in which you were always the giver, that they were nearly devoid of reciprocity. Relationships that literally drained you."

John was listening intently.

"We concluded that there was clearly no material gain and seemingly no emotional gain as well. But was there?"

"What do you mean?"

"Was there an emotional gain? And if so, what was it?"

John pondered the question for a moment or two, then said. "I think it has to do with my father."

"Elaborate."

"Well, my father's leaving left a big hole in my life, but being a young child at the time, I didn't know any other way to fill it other than not making things worse, especially for my mother."

"And how did you do that?"

"By being a good boy all the time, doing what I was told, never asking for anything."

"So, you got used to not asking for anything?"

"I guess so."

"And how did your grandmother reinforce this behavior—your being vigilant about being good and not asking for anything?"

"She did it by comparing me to my father—the bad guy."

"Good insight." I affirmed.

"It's all beginning to make sense. How I got myself all run down."

"Yes. It is. But there's another aspect to it as well. By always doing things

48

for everyone else, not a thought for your own needs and health, what emotional needs were you actually meeting?"

"Being good. Or not being like my father."

"Exactly, John. Exactly. This was a way for you to cope with your loss and its aftermath. And you coped, compensated, well for a long time. You went to an elite high school, found a nice young woman to love as a teen, and served more than honorably in the U.S. Navy and are a tribute to your community. But the world of your childhood, and its great challenges, is in the rearview mirror, you need not use those coping methods anymore."

Bruce Ecker, cofounder of Coherence Therapy, has written extensively about implicit and explicit memories and the role they play in the formation of self-concept (Ecker, et al., 2012). Explicit memories are conscious, long-term memories, easily retrieved. Implicit memories are unconscious—subcortical in their neural configuration and can drive destructive and self-defeating behavior the cause of which an individual is completely unaware. Ecker believes that it is implicit memories—what he calls "consolidated learnings"—that produce the many disturbing symptoms that clients often bring to the attention of mental health professionals. In John's case, his implicit belief was that he was "no good," just like his father. John spent most of his life attempting to disprove this, unknowingly. It nearly killed him.

Over the next two years, John took night and Saturday morning classes in literature, psychology and sociology at a local community college and met a few other veterans taking classes too. He further cultivated his interest in boating and fishing and put his boat—previously sitting for long stretches in his driveway—into the water most seasons and in the process developed a closer relationship with his children. Developing interests and regularly partaking in them, was not only the way in which John countered the behavioral manifestation of the implicit beliefs he grew up with—that he was no good-- but also was a way to teach himself, through repetition, how to become comfortable, syntonic, with having personal needs and fulfilling them. By changing his relationship with himself and with others—consciously creating the conditions for his own growth and development and perhaps of others—John was no longer functioning merely on a compensatory level, but one of self-love (Fromm, 1956).

In total, John and I worked together for nearly four years. The hard therapeutic work took place during the first two years in which John did not have any emotional or behavioral setbacks. He did try to go off his medication twice. Both times, his anxiety returned within weeks. Subsequently, John came to accept that he'd have to continue to take his daily dose of Elavil for the rest of his life.

After I left the mental health center in 1986 and went into private practice, John and I went 32 years without seeing each other, although he sent a few referrals my way. During our last few sessions, he asked that I contact him if I had a book coming out or I was going to do any public speaking locally.

In 2018, I was scheduled to give a lecture on the traumas and types of post-traumatic stress endured by three iconic American authors: J.D. Salinger, Truman Capote and Maya Angelou. Although it never came to pass, we exchanged a few emails and caught up with each other's lives.

John retired from his city job after 30 years. He spends his warmer days in his boat on the waterways of Long Island. He and his wife are well. His two children are thriving professionals, both married, with children. He no longer does jigsaw puzzles but looks back on that assembly of pieces with fond memories.

PostScript

Since John's therapy took place 38 years ago, we had to exchange emails and phone calls to verify, add and sometimes subtract, from the memories we shared of that time so many years ago. We wouldn't have been able to complete the case study without doing so. Our correspondence, particularly over the telephone, was warm and personable and touching, to say the least. It reminded me of the importance of the therapeutic relationship and of the co-evolving nature of it. I grew as a result of my work with John, as much as he did.

John did need medication to balance out his biochemical system—there is much evidence and time to support Dr. Campanella's bold, though nuanced intervention. But the sociobiology of our relationship was as indispensable to John's healing, further growth and development. I'll let John have the last word on that.

"I definitely felt confident with Dr. Campanella, he told me where to start to get better. He told me I would get better, but it would take time. I didn't get sick overnight, so I had to work to get better. Roger, I felt safe with you in our sessions, and you made it easy for me to challenge myself to do what was necessary to get back on an even keel. You were the best friend that I needed to get better, and I thank you from the bottom of my heart for the guidance and love you showed me."

References

Ecker, B., Ticic, R., & Hulley, L. (2012). *Unlocking the Emotional Brain.* Taylor and Francis.

Fromm, E. (1956). *The Art of Loving.* Harper Colophon.

John Hopkins. (n.d.). *Dysthymia.* from https://www.hopkinsmedicine.org/health/conditions-and-diseases/dysthymia.

Levine, P. (1976). *Accumulated stress, reserve capacity, and disease.* University of California.

Mayo Clinic. (n.d.). *Transient ischemic attack (TIA) - Symptoms and causes.* Mayo Clinic. from https://www.mayoclinic.org/diseases-conditions/transient-ischemic-attack/symptoms-causes/syc-20355679.

32-year-old Melissa Triumphs Over Complex Trauma

"What did I get myself into?" I asked myself, as I put my hands over my head and squeezed.

As a child psychotherapist, every once in a while, a case comes your way that seems too much to handle. The client's presenting problems appear to be merely the tip of an emotional iceberg protruding from generations of uninterrupted levels of toxic stress, resulting in emotional instability, family estrangement and poverty.

After meeting with Melissa for well over an hour—to talk about her troubled 12-year-old son in particular and her family in general—I determined that this was such a case. Nonetheless, despite my reservations, I decided to take them on.

Melissa had three children from relationships with three different men. Talbot, the child in question, was the oldest. As she sat across from me, relating her story, she held a month-old baby boy in her arms.

"Talbot's behavior has been difficult at times, but now his grades are going down too."

"What kind of student has Talbot been?" I asked.

"Straight A's. Always at the top of his class."

"And now?"

"C's and D's. He's failing math and social studies."

"Could I get a look at his five-week progress report?"

Melissa removed a manila envelope from her blue baby bag and handed it to me.

I took a look at the report. "I can see what you're talking about."

"I could always depend upon Talbot getting good grades but now…" Melissa began to tear up. "I just don't know what to do."

"It's a tough age, 12, being in junior high. Your body is changing, even your voice. And there are a whole lot of distractions in junior high, unlike elementary school. "

Melissa nodded in agreement, daintily dabbing her eyes with a tissue.

"It's also very hard for a parent," I continued. "So many changes coming at you at once. It's hard to keep up."

Although I believed that Talbot's issues ran deeper than run-of-the mill preteen transgressions, I tried my best to normalize them, make them seem more manageable to Melissa, in the service of our relationship. Given her tumultuous background, I knew that for Talbot's therapy to be successful in the long run, I needed to bond with her and facilitate the process of what the child psychoanalyst D.W. Winnicott referred to as *emotionally holding* (The Child, the Family, and the Outside World, D.W. Winnicott (Middlesex 1973).

Melissa's family profile was complicated, to say the least. She was not only living with the emotionally volatile father of her third child, but her older brother and sister-in-law and their two children. In addition, her younger brother and his on and off girlfriend were also jammed into a four-bedroom duplex apartment, the dimensions of which I was unable to follow, no less envision a family of 11 living there with any semblance of order. No wonder why Talbot was so distressed!

"Talbot has to share a room with his cousin Rob, who's also 12. He's real unhappy about it. They're always fighting about their stuff. But there's nothing we can do about it right now. It's all we can afford, until I get back to work."

I began to see Talbot once a week. He was an engaging, highly articulate, angry young man with a litany of cutting complaints. He'd come into my office, sit on the edge of the couch, lean in and let loose. "My cousin's always stealing my stuff. My money, my games. I wish he'd go back to Baltimore."

Talbot also hated his teachers, his school's assistant principal, his bus driver. "They all have attitude. They're always busting my chops."

"What about your classmates?"

"They're all right. But I like my last school better."

Talbot told me that he had moved several times since kindergarten and has never lived with his biological father. According to Talbot, his father was unreliable, often failing to show up for scheduled visits. "He doesn't have a job and lives with my grandmother. He's a real loser."

"What about your mother's present boyfriend?"

"He's an asshole. I can't believe my mother stays with him. He's always in a bad mood. He's always yelling at us."

"What makes you happy? Brings you enjoyment."

"Being alone. Playing my games." Talbot had the latest video game systems but was forbidden by his mother to play on the internet, so he couldn't develop any online friendships like "normal" kids.

As the weeks went by and little changed in his life, particularly regarding where and how he lived, Talbot, understandably, began to resist coming to sessions. Since I believed that Talbot needed a steady and stable relationship with a healthy, dependable male, I did my best to keep him in therapy. His mother gave me permission to take him to the Dunkin Donuts shop near my office. Over donuts and hot chocolate, we talked about family life and school. But by about his sixth month of therapy, he refused to come into my office.

"He's sitting in the car. He refuses to come in." Melissa had called me from the parking lot.

"Can you come in for a few minutes?"

"Sure."

When she entered my office, I asked "Where's the baby?" I had gotten used to seeing him with her in the waiting room and was taking great pleasure in his growth and development. "He's home—with his dad. Robert had the day off."

Melissa proceeded to tell me that Talbot's grades had recovered considerably from their first quarter nose-dive, but he was getting impossible to live with. "All he does is complain and make nasty remarks to me and his sister. I wish his father was more stable, so I could send him over there, give me *and* him a break."

"Yeah. You could probably use one."

After a brief silence, Melissa asked, "So, what can we do? I can't physically drag him in here."

"Would you consider coming to see me by yourself? I can help you help Talbot."

"I would like that. I've always felt that I could use some therapy myself."

"Very good." I replied.

After working out an appointment time for Melissa, I asked. "Would it be all right if I went out to the car and spoke to Talbot about how we're proceeding? I'll bring him a donut."

"I think he'd really like that. I mean, that you're going out to speak with him. Not the donut." We both laughed.

When I got out to the car, Talbot had his headphones on, a pencil in his hand, a school notebook in his lap. I motioned for him to roll down the car window.

"Hi Talbot," I said. "Your mom says that you don't want to continue our sessions. That's perfectly understandable. Nothing's really changed for you at home. I wish I could have accomplished more. I've really grown to like you. I care about you very much."

"Thank you." Talbot said.

"You're welcome." I smiled. "So, this is what we're going to do. I'm going to work with your mom every week and try to make things better-with your living situation."

I persuaded Talbot to come into the office, "just for a few minutes" to settle things with his mom.

It didn't take long for Talbot to start complaining about his cousin Rob, his noisy baby brother.

"You don't like anything Talbot. Nothing will please you." Melissa retorted.

"But mommy. But mommy…" He was pleading with his mother to understand.

Melissa reached over and pulled him close. "I'm sorry about how things have turned out. I promise to work with Roger to make them better."

It was at this moment that I felt deep in my heart that I could help this mother and son get better, heal their wounds, however deep. I was stirred by the tenderness shared between them. Just think—a nearly 13-year-old boy, on the surface, a tough boy, an angry boy, calling his mother *mommy*. Even more, his mother sensing his vulnerability and responding to it with such warmth and sensitivity. I was now all in, in more ways than one.

As alluded to earlier, Melissa's background, her history of emotional, social, and economic turmoil, supported the belief that her son Talbot was merely the manifestation a much deeper disturbance in the larger family system. For one, Melissa's mother, Marilyn had been married and divorced five times by the time Melissa was 22. Like her son Talbot, she had never had a steady, stable, paternal figure in her life. Adding insult to psychic injury, Melissa's maternal grandmother, Mattie, appeared to have little interest in her children, preferring to work a full-time job, leaving her many children, Melissa's aunts, and uncles, to fend for themselves. Children who grow up in these kinds of circumstances begin to develop the expectation that even their most basic emotional needs will not be met, especially when a father or grandparent doesn't step in and take over the role of child-rearing to compensate for an uninvolved or absent mother. This type of intergenerational emotional deprivation is a recipe for disaster in more ways than one.

According to the evolutionary biologist, Dr. Haley Peckham, this kind of early and ongoing emotional neglect leads to profound life-shaping worldviews and maladaptive attachment styles of enduring consequence. Dr. Peckham posits that the biological imperative is to reproduce yourself before you die; that severe early neglect and abuse promotes an unconscious feeling of impending morbidity. Therefore, if you believe that you're going to die young, your desire to reproduce yourself, to procreate, will be intense and persistent until it's fulfilled. Unfortunately, this leads to too many teenagers and young adults having children before they are equipped to take care of them emotionally and support them economically.

This strongly suggested that Melissa and her mother both felt threatened by forces inside and outside of them and subsequently were compelled to mate early and often, producing nine children between them, well before either one of them was prepared or equipped to raise or support them. This left Melissa, like her mother, dependent on a series of men who often treated them poorly and abused and neglected their children, perpetuating the intergenerational toxic cycle.

During our first few sessions, Melissa often voiced how difficult it was to contend with Talbot's barrage of complaints and criticisms, especially when they were directed at his younger sister and baby brother.

"It's almost non-stop. Sometimes I think I'm going crazy. I'm always nervous around him"

"Where does your boyfriend Robert fit into all of this?"

"He's always yelling at Talbot and threatens to hit him."

"Does Robert ever hit the children?"

"He's tried. But I get in the way."

"Has Robert hit you?"

"We've hit each other."

"Are you safe?"

"Physically. But not emotionally. That's why I'm here."

"Ok. But if you ever feel you or the kids are in danger—for any reason—call the police, remove yourself from the situation and call me. I'll help arrange temporary housing for you."

O.K.," Melissa somberly replied.

Notice that I did not recommend that Melissa gather up her children and take flight from Robert and her chaotic household of family members. I already knew that Melissa had lived in a shelter with Talbot when he was a baby and she vowed never to end up in a shelter again.

"I was always worried for our safety there," she'd said. "In some ways it's worse than being in an abusive relationship."

Melissa also stated that with her brothers around, she was certain that Robert wouldn't get out of hand and hurt anyone. Nonetheless, fearing for the family's safety, I decided to stick out my therapeutic neck even further.

"Do you think Robert would be willing to come in to see me?" I asked.

"I'm pretty sure he would"

"Really?" I was surprised by her response.

"He thinks the therapy is good for me. He thinks Talbot shouldn't have been allowed to stop, particularly when he saw that he was doing better in school and getting up in the morning without too much of a fuss."

"I see?"

"I know that I have portrayed Robert mostly negatively. But there's another side of him. He really cares, wants things to get better. He'd do just about anything for us."

"Is that why you got involved with him in the first place?"

"Yes," Melissa replied affirmatively.

Robert was a tall, thick oak tree of a man, with long light brown hair and gentle blue eyes. Despite his line of work, his hands were still soft, although his handshake was firm.

"I'm a 'horticulturist,'" Robert said sarcastically, making air quotes with his two long fingers.

"'I see,'" I said, mimicking Robert's air quotes.

Robert laughed. "I climb trees, cut, prune, slap on some medicine."

"How's that working out for you?"

"It pays the bills."

Robert actually ran a crew of 12 men who worked long hard days between March and October.

"Do you get to take a break during the down months?"

"Nah." Robert shook his head. "I go around fixing landscaping equipment. Tractors, wood-chippers, rototillers. Whatever needs fixing."

"Wow. Where'd you learn how to do all this?"

"Working summers, weekends during high school."

"Did you go to college?" I already knew he hadn't.

"No way."

"How come? Sounds like you could have gotten a degree in engineering."

"That's what they tell me." Robert replied.

Robert confirmed Melissa's claims that he had done extremely well when in high school, taking advanced math and science classes and graduating a year early.

Robert leaned forward in his chair. "Regarding school—the fact of the matter is, Dr. K.—is that I just don't like people. They annoy the hell out of me."

He suddenly sounded like a character out of J.D. Salinger's "The Catcher in the Rye," but I resisted the urge to lean forward and reply, "All right, Holden."

During the next couple of sessions with Robert, I learned some troubling facts. Robert was on a cocktail of antipsychotics, prescribed by a local psychiatrist who was not known for being easy with the prescription pad.

"They really tire me out," Robert was referring to the meds. "Sometimes I have to knock down a couple of Redbulls to stay awake."

"Next session, bring in all the bottles of the medications you're taking so we can go over them."

I was actually trying to verify what Robert was claiming, so I wouldn't have to contact his psychiatrist and complicate matters more than I already had. It turned out that Robert was actually taking enough anti-psychotics to tranquilize a herd of horses and his psychiatrist most likely believed that he was potentially dangerous.

Subsequently, my bimonthly therapy sessions with Robert had to be part therapist, part security guard. I would show a great deal of interest in his work, explore his relationships and interactions with coworkers, landscape customers and the people he was living with, while gauging whether or not his temperature valve was ready to blow.

"I've only heard Melisa's and Talbot's side of the story." I told him.

"Well," Robert said with rising intensity. "What pisses me off most is the way she lets her kids walk all over her. I bust my ass climbing trees all day and come home to endless bickering."

"And what about Melissa's siblings?"

"Don't get me started. Her sister-in-law's a maniac. Always starting trouble. But her eldest brother Steven is ok. Him and I are in the same boat. We're involved with two women who can't control their freaking kids. I can't wait to get us out of there!"

"Any plans?"

Robert nodded. "I'm going to ask my boss for a raise."

Robert was making only 24 dollars an hour. He was extremely underpaid for a young man of his skills, technical knowhow, and supervisory responsibilities.

"I know a guy that gets 40 per hour to run a crew like yours. 50 hours in, gets you 100K a year, plus tips."

"He won't give me 40, but maybe 34."

"You'd be worth every penny and more."

"Thanks," Robert replied.

After working with Melissa a few months, one to two sessions a week, I decided to raise a sensitive issue, indirectly.

"With all the stress you've experienced these last few years, how is your overall health?" I asked.

"Pretty bad. I'm way overweight and completely embarrassed by the way I look. I've gained over a 100 pounds since I gave birth to Talbot."

Melissa took out her phone and proceeded to show me a picture of herself. "I was about 21 or so."

"Nice," I replied.

As a younger woman Melissa had been petite and shapely, with long beautiful blonde hair down to the small of her back.

"No matter what I do, no matter how I try, I just can't seem to drop the weight. I just keep get bigger and bigger. I'm disgusted with myself."

"You're not alone," I answered. "It's very hard to lose weight—get healthy—when you're under so much duress."

Melissa went on to say that her weight had caused her great physical pain because her thin, petite frame—she was five foot two and well over 200 pounds—couldn't bear the pounds with which it was presently burdened.

"I'm so embarrassed over how I've let myself go that I haven't gone to a doctor in years."

"Even a gynecologist?"

"Well, yes. I had to leading up to the little one's birth. But I never go to a regular doctor, ever."

I paused in thought. "What if you went to a doctor to treat your depression? To get medicine. This way you wouldn't have to go through a physical examination."

"You don't think therapy is enough?"

"I think that therapy can help to some extent. But you have indicated that you've been depressed and anxious as long as you can remember, as well as your mother. When a depression reaches or better put, descends to a level of illness, medicine is required to improve the effectiveness of therapy."

"I see," Mellissa replied.

"Could you call your insurance company and see if they're any providers that I know and get back to me?"

"Okay." Melissa nodded.

A few days later, Melissa phoned to say that she took the initiative to call several psychiatrists listed on the provider website, but none of them were taking her insurance or hadn't called her back.

"Keep calling," I told her, hoping to provide support to her initiative. "Something will work out."

As the weeks passed by, it appeared that Melissa wasn't going to be able to get an appointment with a psychiatrist or nurse practitioner using her health insurance and couldn't afford to pay large fees out of pocket.

"I know why they're not returning my calls. It's because I have the government insurance. It took me months to find you."

"It's very discouraging," I replied sympathetically.

I knew that it was crucially important for Melissa to see a psychiatrist and get a proper medication evaluation for her depression. It was very clear that at least in part, Melissa ate because she was depressed, and she was depressed because she ate. If she didn't treat her depression at its neurophysiological core, it was likely that she wouldn't be able to lose the excess pounds that were causing her so much psychic and physical pain and prevented her from even believing that she could one day begin to explore the heights of her potential.

What to do? I had become very fond of Melissa and struggled to deal with my paternal feelings toward her. I believed that the care and sensitivity that she demonstrated toward her three children, in spite of never receiving that kind of care herself when a child and teenager, indicated that there was something unique, something special about her. I thought that with the right kind of help she could become a much healthier and happier young woman.

At our next session, after resolving not to secretly pay a psychiatrist to see her—an outrageous example of countertransference, if there ever was one—I said to Melissa. "Let me see what I can do. You might have to travel a bit, but I think I can find someone that takes your insurance."

"If you say so," Melissa was not optimistic.

"Try to keep the faith. There are people out there that want to help you."

"O.K." A child-like smile broke out on Melissa's face.

There was a health clinic a few miles from my home, where I received my own health care. I had a good relationship with the staff. When I inquired about Melissa's health insurance, they said that they accepted it and that she should call and make an appointment with the nurse practitioner.

The next session, I provided Melissa with the information that she needed to make an appointment.

"It's real far away. I'll have to have someone go with me," she said.

A week later, a few days before her appointment, her friend backed out of going with her. Her boyfriend Robert, understandably skeptical of prescribers of psychotropic medicine, was discouraging her from going.

"What if you started out real early and I met you there?" I asked.

"You would?"

"Yes. It's my day off. I don't live too far from the clinic."

I had Melissa fill out a few forms giving me permission to meet her at the clinic and to talk to the nurse practitioner after she was done seeing her.

A day later, I received a call from Robert. "It was very nice of you to offer to meet Melissa at the clinic. That's way beyond the call of duty. I going to take the afternoon off from work and drive her over there. Thanks for all your help."

"You're doing a real good thing Robert. I real good thing. I'll make sure she's not overmedicated."

"Thank you."

My offer to meet Melissa at the health clinic was questionable—perhaps an expression of counter-transference over-reach. An intervention of this kind, however well-meaning, not only risked imposing on Melissa, the client, more help than she actually needed but could promote an unhealthy dependency on me. In other words, my overreach was likely a projection of my need, not hers, to get better, at this stage in her therapy, not mine.

Psychotherapists, with varying degrees of experience, grapple with feelings of counter transference—feelings they have toward their clients. We struggle to manage these feelings appropriately and professionally and learn how to use them effectively. In rare cases, therapists have too little or too many feelings toward a client initially, and it's therefore better to refer them to someone more suitable.

It didn't take me long to discover, with the help of a trusted colleague, the sources of my counter transferential feelings toward Melissa, old and new. It begins with the old age frustration that many therapists share—the inability to have any positive impact on the mental health of those closest to us, in my case, my older siblings and my mother. Also, my long-held belief that if I had had a younger sibling to love and care for, to shower with gifts and affection, I would have been a much happier child and young adult. Melissa obviously fit the bill.

I vowed to modulate my paternal feelings toward her more mindfully and productively and to continue to discuss them with my colleague on a regular basis, lest I risk undermining the whole therapeutic enterprise.

Melissa did meet with a doctor at the health clinic. She received a diagnosis of dysthymia, a low grade but chronic form of depression, consistent with her symptoms. I was pleased to hear that the doctor spent over an hour with her, getting a detailed intergenerational history and administering a thorough, yet uninvasive physical examination. Melissa let the doctor know that she was experiencing pain in certain parts of her body, particularly in her lower back. She believed that some of her pain was related to her depression, and some to her weight gain.

Melissa was prescribed the anti-depressant Lexapro, what I had hoped for, because it treated back and nerve pain, as well as depression. It also did not contain a stimulant. Sometimes symptoms appear to be the result of an underlying depressive illness, but are actually a bipolar disorder, especially when the client presents with a great deal of anxiety. Giving an anti-depressant, such as Wellbutrin (which does contain a stimulant), to a person with a bipolar or an anxiety disorder, could make them worse and set in motion a seemingly endless and tragic search for the "right" antidepressant when the client was actually suffering from a different underlying illness.

Within a month, Melissa was feeling better, without any significant side effects. "My anxiety is completely gone. Nothing seems to trigger it. And I'm less achy. But I still feel very tired. I'm not motivated to do anything. Sometimes, after the kids are off to school and the baby is sleeping, I stare off into space. I'm way behind in housework. But I do feel better." Melissa chuckled.

We proceeded to look up the side effects of Lexapro on our cell phones.

"It looks like one of the side effects is tiredness, brain fog. When are you seeing the doctor next? Maybe the dosage can be adjusted."

"That's what I thought."

During Melissa's next visit with the doctor, something surprising and unusual happened. The doctor told Melissa that she was pleased with her progress and that she didn't need to adjust her dosage of the Lexapro because her bloodwork suggested that something else might be preventing her from achieving a more fully therapeutic effect of the drug. It turned out that Melissa had a significant vitamin D deficit—which explained why her mood hadn't improved--and was immediately prescribed a potent dose Vitamin D. Prescription level doses of Vitamin D are more effective than store bought over the counter Vitamin D supplements because the body absorbs them more effectively.

Within three weeks of starting the Vitamin D regiment, Melissa's mood was on the upswing and her ability to focus improved immensely.

"I'm no longer painfully peeling myself out of bed each morning. I'm getting the kids off to school without much of a problem."

"Fantastic!" I smiled.

"I can't believe I feel so good. I hope it lasts."

"It will," I replied. "But you can help it along."

"How?"

"Well, your energy level is like a purring engine in idle. It's waiting for you to step on the gas and go somewhere."

"What do you mean?"

"Now that you have all this energy, besides getting out of bed each morning and getting the kids off to school, what would you like to do for yourself? What are you interested in?"

"I would love to decorate."

"Sounds good to me."

"But my sister-in-law will get in the way. She'll think I'm trying to take over or something."

"I'm sure you'll be able to figure something out."

"The best solution is to move out. I'm tired of sharing the house with her."

"Any plans?"

"Just waiting to see if Robert gets the raise he's asking for. That would be a great help."

I nodded in agreement.

When a body gets a surge of energy, when it's poised to emerge from a long, dispiriting depressive slumber, it needs to find a place in which to channel that new-found energy productively. Developing an interest in something, particularly something new, will serve to stimulate the parts of the brain that have remained dormant due to disuse. Depressed patients tend to have problems with mental functioning, particularly with long-term memory, not because the memories have faded or have been displaced by others, but because the mental mechanisms to retrieve the memory have become deconditioned. Planned task-oriented activities can aide a patient's recovery from a depressive illness not only by creating new long-term and functional memories to draw from, but also by rebalancing brain system activity. Spending more time in the executive network of the brain, away from previous default mode network dominance (where all the unproductive mind wandering takes place) is an avenue toward better mental health, (John Arden, Mind-Brain-Gene: Toward Psychotherapy Integration, Norton & Norton Inc., 2019.)

During the next three months, the focus of Melissa's therapy sessions changed dramatically. She spoke little of her son Talbot and her boyfriend Robert, but more so about herself and her background.

"It's hard to believe that I dropped out of high school at 16 and nobody did anything about it."

"Nobody? Not even the school social worker?"

"No. I was in special ed with the rest of the losers, and nobody gave a damn."

"You were in special ed? How did you end up in special ed?"

"I had problems learning. I couldn't focus. I was a nervous wreck."

This revelation, on Melissa's part, was extraordinary. The neglect and lack of supervision on the part of her parents and the school district was one thing, but the need for small classroom supportive educational services was quite another.

"But you're so articulate," I asserted. "You use language with such....exactitude."

"If you say so." Melissa remained unconvinced.

"So why do you think you had such difficulties in school?"

"I was very self-conscious. I sat in the back of the room, away from everyone. I never raised my hand, even if I knew the answer. I didn't want to draw any attention to myself in anyway."

"How come?"

"I hated the way I looked. I was over developed in the chest area and boys were always staring at me, making stupid comments. It was intolerable."

"It sure sounded like it. But I bet if you weren't so anxious your natural intelligence, just like your son's and daughter's, would have come out."

"A lot that has gotten me." Melissa was still anchored to beliefs about herself that weren't true.

I pushed on. "What do you mean?"

"Well, no matter how articulate, no matter how much natural intelligence I might have, where has it gotten me. I have no diplomas to speak of and the only job I've ever had was cleaning and painting rental apartments."

"Would you like to get your high school diploma?"

"Yes. I would. But I have so much to make up."

"Maybe. Maybe not. Would you like me to look into it for you?"

"Sure." Melissa perked up. "What do I have to lose?"

Regarding Melissa's time in school, she couldn't recall whether or not her mother signed her out at 16, or school authorities lost track of her during one of her many moves. I instructed Melissa to contact the last high school that she had attended and request a copy of her school records. If she had not been declassified from receiving special education services before leaving school, she would be considered disabled by New York State and would be entitled to free remedial educational services and or vocational training, even at 32 years old.

But obtaining her records from the school district proved a formidable task. Remarkably, the high school claimed to not have them and referred her to the administrative offices. Once there, Melissa was informed that the district shredded and disposed of all records after seven years.

"That just doesn't seem right. Do you suspect something?"

"Yeah. The record of how all of us special ed kids were quote un quate "educated.""

"How does that make you feel?"

"Angry! Like I want to get back at them!"

"In what way?" I was still concerned that if Robert finds out about the school district's intransigence, he might do something impulsive out of anger.

"Sue the bastards!"

I liked the way this was going for Melissa emotionally, although there was little standing for educational malpractice suits in New York State. Melissa's newfound ability to confront her terribly stressful past, by returning to the proverbial scene of the crime—her high school and the school district's administrative offices—was a sign of strength, an emotional challenge she wouldn't have been able to face while in the throes of her long-standing depression. She was also beginning to piece together a coherent narrative of how she became the person is she, not only how she perceived but conceived of herself, a self with which she was becoming increasingly in conflict.

"Since the school district isn't going to help, as I expected, I'm going to have to have a talk with my mother, maybe my biological father and aunt."

"Good luck." I said half- jokingly.

Melissa and I began to laugh a bit more heartily than expected, our eyes mirroring our mutual degree of skepticism.

It turned out that Melissa's mother Marilyn had signed her out of school after all but couldn't find the paperwork to prove it.

"She became all defensive, which was surprising, like she actually cared," Melissa stated. "She said that I was pleading with her to sign me out of that god forsaken place as soon as I reached my 16th birthday. On that exact day."

"Do you believe her?"

"Yes. And no. I believe that I begged her to sign me out. But I don't believe she cared."

"Do you think she had other motives?"

"Well, to get me and the school district off her back—while she was going on and off the marriage merry-go-round. If I wasn't in school, I could be home and help raise her younger children. I've been taking care of my younger brother practically since he was born. He's 18 and still with me."

I had the urge to say to Melissa, "God bless you," for being such a good sister. "God bless you." But I resisted, not wanting to risk communicating the wrong affirmation, however well meaning.

"What about this aunt of yours that you refer to on occasion. What side of the family is she on?" I decided to go in a different direction to get to the same place.

"She's my mother's sister. She was always very kind to me. Always helping me out with my brother. Bringing us food, clothes. I love her dearly."

"Could it be that it was she was the adult in your life who provided you with a role model of caring for others, as you do so well with your own children?"

"Probably. I can't think of anyone else."

I had recently finished my first 21 hours of training in hypnosis. I was not interested in becoming a certified hypnotist. I was more interested in the science of the hypnotic process and how to help my clients achieve a deeper level of relaxation without putting them in a trance. I decided that this was the right time to set up a suggestion sequence that might lead to the possibility of doing deeper work later on in the therapy, if Melissa so allowed.

"There are three things that the human race's survival is dependent on," I started, keeping on the theme of caring for others. "First, the protection of our offspring. Second, the nurturing of our offspring. Third, the cooperation with our offspring. Without those three things, the human race's chances of survival would be greatly reduced."

Melissa sat quietly, yet intently listening.

"To protect, to nurture, to cooperate. It seems so simple. Enjoyable. How could anyone think of doing anything other?"

Melissa began to laugh.

"But they do. It's as if they're acting against their own good nature."

A few months later, Robert's boss granted him a $10 an hour raise and promised to pay him time and the half on Saturdays. This increase in revenue allowed the family to move into a small rental house. Melissa's brother, sister-in-law and their children moved back to Baltimore. Melissa's younger brother and his girlfriend rented a room down the block from the new home. This was a positive move for Melissa and her immediate family in several ways. It gave her and Robert the degree of privacy a young couple raising a toddler needed and provided Talbot, now 14, with a room of his own for the first time in three years. It also gave Melissa free rein over her home in which she could decorate as she pleased. Most families take these conditions for granted, but these were profound changes for Melissa.

But there were challenges as well, particularly when it came to the management of the children. Melissa argued that Robert was too harsh in his attempts to guide or discipline them; while Robert believed that Melissa allowed them to regularly disrespect her wishes, that Melissa was a "pushover." I attempted to work out a compromise between them through a few couple's therapy sessions, but the sessions were so acrimonious, so full of rancor, as to render them unproductive therapeutically.

"Can we at least agree on one thing?" I asked them.

"I'll try," Melissa said somewhat sarcastically.

"Since Talbot is starting high school next week and getting up before everyone else, I'm recommending that Robert take charge of getting him off to school so you can get some more sleep."

I turned to Robert. "No yelling, no threats. Make direct eye contact with Talbot, all body language in the direction of the bathroom, kitchen, etc....Supervise his morning routine from the moment he's supposed to wake up and out the door to the bus stop. Capeesh?"

"Capeesh." Robert smiled.

I worked out this agreement between Melissa and Robert for several reasons. For one, it seemed to be an arrangement with which they could comply, likely to result in a successful outcome. It also provided Melissa with an opportunity to sleep a few more hours and not have to start off her day stressfully trying to get resistant 14-year-old Talbot out of bed. But most importantly, with Robert supervising, Talbot would get off to school regularly, reducing the risk of him falling behind academically and following in his family's footsteps by dropping out of high school prematurely.

Over the next three or four months, Melissa focused her newfound energy on improving her health. She tried several different diets and began to go on morning walks, pushing her baby boy Jason, now two-years-old, in his stroller to a nearby rocky beach. Melissa did best when she was joined by a friend or a cousin in her weight loss pursuits. But when they stumbled, fell off the proverbial weight loss wagon, she slipped as well.

"It's so frustrating," Melissa said. "Every time I give birth, I gain more weight and I'm never able to take it off."

"Maybe we should focus more on exercise and stress response and the weight loss will come." I was trying to remain upbeat.

"All right," she replied, still sounding defeated.

During the next few weeks, I explained and demonstrated various stress reduction methods for Melissa to use to minimize the degree to which she used food as a means to reduce stress. We practiced various breathing techniques and a few counting and tapping approaches. Melissa would be able to apply them for weeks of a time, lose weight, but then would back track and regain the weight. It seemed as if nothing was going to work.

The morning of one of our scheduled session, Melissa called to ask if we could conduct our session over the phone.

"Sure," I replied. "Are you ok? Is everything all right?"

"Not exactly. But I'm not sick, if that's what you're asking. You'll know why when we talk."

"O.K., I answered.

I was not concerned that Melissa was considering ending her therapy and couldn't face telling me in person, although therapists do have blind spots, miss cues that in retrospective might have been obvious. But Melissa faithfully attended all her sessions and was an active participate in all of them. Also, her investment in the therapeutic alliance, our relationship, was substantial, for it extended well beyond her emotionally needs to include those of her entire family. For over two years, my presence in their livres had provided them with a modicum of order and safety in the face of a too often tenuous presence and perilous future.

When I called, Melissa took her time answering the phone.

"Hi," she said.

"Hi," my voice was soft.

"This is very difficult. I need some time," her voice was cracking.

"Take all the time you need."

Melissa appeared to be sipping some water before she hesitatingly began.

"I've always thought that I should speak to someone about this, but I wasn't confident enough to tell anyone—no offense to you—because I didn't trust anyone. Robert doesn't even know about this."

"I take no offense."

There appeared to be more sipping of water on Melissa's end.

"When I was 12, I was raped…twice." (Even as I write this years later, my eyes begin to well up in tears.)

"How terrible, Melissa. How terrible." Upon hearing this, my chest had tightened in pain.

"It was a friend of the family. He was left behind to look after me after my mother and stepfather went out with her friends. I was a very developed 12-year-old. He told me that I would like it and forced me to take off all my clothes. I was terrified, but I at least had the presence of mind to ask him to wrap his penis in saran wrap so he wouldn't impregnant me. I was already menstruating."

"How awful. How awful," is all I could say.

"I told my mother and stepfather about it. He denied it and they didn't believe me. Two weeks later, they sent him to a house where I was baby-sitting a relative's kid. He had offered to drive me home. As usual, my mother and stepfather were busy partying or something. I objected but they said I had to go with him. On the ride to my house, he pulled off to the side of the road and forced me to cover his penis with my mouth. It was even more disgusting than my vagina being penetrated."

There was a short pause. "I have to drink some water," Melissa said.

"Go right ahead. Please take your time. This is very difficult to talk about."

After a few minutes of silence, Melissa began again. "I didn't even tell anyone about the second time. I was just contented with not having to be alone with this guy ever again. I guess the reason I brought this up, other than the obvious reasons, is that I moved back into the neighborhood I grew up and he lives there. He's probably in his 50's."

"Are you afraid that you might see him?"

"Yes and no. I want him to pay for what he did, but I'd afraid of him and I don't know what I'd do if I actually saw him. I could blind side him. He wouldn't recognize me 22 years later."

"You're not alone in these feelings. I admire your ability to come forth with this. It takes a lot of strength to share—with anyone—such a horrific experience."

"Thank you," Melissa replied.

With this tragic revelation, there was much for Melissa and me to process. Although her childhood neglect set her up for a volatile adolescence and young adulthood, the trauma she endured at the hands of a rapist was most likely the cause of her present emotional dysregulation. Traumatic experiences differ from painful ones in that trauma causes injury to the autonomic nervous system and results in varying degrees of stress response impairment. Would a closer look at Melissa's day to day activities reveal symptoms of post-traumatic stress?

"Before I started seeing you, I lived a reclusive life. I rarely went out by myself. I had to wait for Robert to come home from work to go food shopping, sometimes he had to go with me to the doctor for the kid's check-ups. But I never attributed it to what that guy did to me. I thought I was just ashamed of the way I looked and very anxious in general and needed company."

"What about your handling of the kids?" I already knew the answer to the question.

"Well, before we started seeing you, I wouldn't allow them to go to other kids houses. They always had to come to us."

"And what about you and Robert? Did you ever socialize with other couples, friends? Not spending any time with other adults can drive you crazy as well."

"We just started doing that now. Every other Wednesday night we go to Robert's boss' house and spend some time with his coworkers."

"How has that gone for you?"

"At first, I just stood around with a drink in my hand saying nothing, thinking about how big I was compared to the other woman. But after a while I realized that no one cared and I began to loosen up, join the conversation."

Melissa had certainly been suffering from the symptoms of post-traumatic stress and probably still was. The prominent symptom appeared to be hypervigilance, evidenced by the way in which she erected barriers between herself and, later on, her children and the outside world. No wonder why she selected a mate like Robert, a man, that was at the ready to defend himself against threats even when there were mostly none. They were a couple mostly at unease with the world, Melissa ready to withdraw, *flee*, Robert to attack, *fight*. The amygdala, the part of the reptilian brain, where the flight, fight or freeze mechanism was located, was primed for activation in Melissa and Robert alike. Afterall, the essence of the post-traumatic life is an inability to sustain a period of calm or relaxation, without assistance. Melissa mostly used food to achieve short term emotional equilibrium, Robert a cocktail of anti-psychotics and nicotine.

An outgrowth of Melissa revealing that she had been sexually assaulted twice at 12-years-old, was a more frank, more serious discussion of sexual matters than we had had before.

"I really don't like it." Melissa giggled. "Although I've had my share of it."

"What don't you like about it?"

"I find it all perverse, disgusting!"

"How come?"

"Well, there's the rapes. But there's also my mother and all those men that came in and out of our lives. I've also checked some of my mother's social media profiles. Pretty perverse. Leather outfits, belts, sex objects. Stuff like that."

"Sadomasochism?"

"I believe so." Melissa sighed.

Melissa went on to say that besides viewing sex as not being tender or loving physically, she hated her body, couldn't stand to look at her body naked.

"But Robert? He doesn't mind at all. He even thinks that my attempts at dieting or exercising to lose weight are foolhardy. What I look like doesn't matter to him. Sometimes I wish I were involved with someone who gave a hoot, who wanted me to slim back down to the shape I was in when we met. But with this body and my attitude toward sex, who would want me?"

It saddened me to hear Melissa talk about herself in this way, but perhaps digging down deeper to the ground zero of her bruised and battered self-esteem could provide an opportunity to cultivate a firmer, more vibrant foundation.

"Do you know," I began. "That thousands, perhaps millions of women who have had your experiences feel the same exact way?"

"What do you mean?"

"Well, when you spoke of your negative attitude toward sex and your size—that no man would be attracted to you because of it."

"Right."

"Well, women who have problems losing, but especially sustaining healthy weight loss often have been sexually assaulted. They *don't* want men to be attracted to them. It triggers their fear of being assaulted again."

Melissa was quietly, intently listening.

"There was a study done in California between 1995 and 1997. It was called the ACE Survey. ACE stands for Adverse Childhood Experiences. The higher the score the more likely a person will have significant physical and mental health problems in adulthood."

Melissa was solemnly nodding her head in agreement.

"Do you know how the study came about?"

"How?"

"Through prejudice and discrimination against people like you, women who were sexually assaulted who were not believed or not taken as seriously as they should have been."

"What? What?" Melissa was in disbelief.

"*What* is right!" I replied. "Let me explain."

"This renowned, incredibly dedicated physician, Dr. Vincent Felliti, was running a weight loss program for mostly very overweight people in California. For five years, half of the patients dropped out, despite the fact they were doing well, but weren't near to completing the program."

"This was very troubling to Dr. Felitti, and he was determined to get to the bottom of it. He and his colleagues reviewed the files of 500 people who had dropped out of the program prematurely. Two hundred and eighty-six of the participants were eventually reinterviewed. It was revealed that most of them had been sexually assaulted in childhood and believed that by remaining overweight, remaining *fat*, they could protect themselves, keep men at a distance, by being unattractive."

"Sounds right." Melissa nodded.

I went onto explain that when Dr. Felliti presented his findings to a conference of obesity specialists, his research was roundly and rudely rejected. One so-called obesity expert stood up and told Dr. Felitti that he "was naive to believe his patients, that it was commonly understood by those more familiar with such matters that these patient statements were fabrications to provide a cover explanation for failed lives."

"Unbelievable," Melissa said.

"Fortunately, a representative from the Centers for Disease Control and Prevention was there, and he invited Dr. Felitti to expand his research to the general public. Ultimately, 17000 adults in the San Diego area participated in the study and it was proven, beyond a reasonable doubt, that adverse childhood experiences result in significant physical and mental health problems later in life, compared to those who experienced little or no adversity in childhood."

"I have a lot to think about," Melissa said.

"Me too," I replied.

Over the next several months, Melissa used this new-found knowledge derived from the ACE Survey as a springboard to talk about her sexual assault more openly and freely. She explored how it shaped and negatively impacted her body image and her attitude toward sex. It was one thing if she didn't care for certain aspects of her anatomy like most people. Or that she was more or less inclined toward sexual activity in general. Those choices on Melissa's part would be voluntary. But this type of distorted thinking was the result of trauma, not a thoughtful, realistic appraisal of one's anatomy or sexual inclinations.

One of the positive changes that resulted from Melissa's addressing her traumatic past more directly, was that the intensity of her fear diminished, and she became less guarded toward the outside world. She started going food shopping on her own and spent time at a local coffee shop with her cousin. She even sponsored a Pampered Chef party in her dining room, no longer fearful or ashamed of having people in her home. When with people, particularly outside of her home, she employed a social engagement strategy to counter sympathetic nervous system triggering and its counterpart, hypervigilance, by being well-mannered and friendly to the people she encountered in parking lots, supermarket aisles and check-out counters. Positive social engagement with others turns on the parasympathetic nervous system, promoting calm and feelings of well-being, by stimulating the vagal nerve, (Porges, 2011).

An equally important indication of Melissa's less fretful engagement with the world, was her willingness to take her son Jason to the playground and allowing her middle child, now 10-years-old, to visit other children's houses for play dates, occasionally sleep over. This was no small feat for someone who had been so vigilant in her attempt to protect herself from a world she perceived as highly threatening.

When providing therapy to clients who have experienced trauma, whether the client reported the trauma during the first few sessions, or as in the case of Melissa, it was revealed much later in therapy, the treating therapist is faced with many challenges. How should the therapy proceed from there? What interventions should be considered?

More in-depth trauma work is typically commenced after the client's symptoms of post-traumatic stress have been significantly reduced and a program of self-care is in place. To borrow from Mike Dubi's helpful metaphor, "A client needs to start off in the shallow end of the pool before they can swim in deeper waters." Also, the distorted and in many cases, dissociated thinking that arises out of traumatic experiences needs to be addressed and reprocessed cognitively. In the case of Melissa, she was no longer experiencing the symptoms of post-traumatic stress. As long as she continued to take her daily doses of Lexapro and her weekly Vitamin D supplement, her depressive illness was kept at bay and her energy level was more than adequate. As described in detail before, Melissa's recent behavior strongly suggested that she believed that the world outside her home was safe enough to risk a more robust engagement.

We discussed two different interventions. The first intervention, that would take direct aim at her sexual assault and the man who committed it, is often referred to as *negative visualization*. Negative visualization is a method by which a client conjures anxiety provoking images and addresses them, from a safe distance, usually within the confines of a trusted therapist's office. I have done negative visualization with several clients and with myself, with much success. In Melissa's case, through the use of a guided meditation, I would help her achieve a state of deep relaxation. Once so physically disposed, she would be free to conjure the image of the man who assaulted her and speak to him in any way she chose, all the while triggering bound up traumatic energy and discharging it in a controlled, measured manner through biofeedback techniques she had already mastered. The goal of negative visualization, shared with other trauma treatment approaches, is to help a client safely decouple the traumatic memory from the embedded traumatic energy, resulting in partial or complete neurological resolution of the experience.

The other intervention, a version of the Weitzman Relaxation Induction, was less direct, yet could still address Melissa's sexual assault and her childhood neglect as well. The Weitzman *Induction* is often used as a first step in the hypnotic process, followed by the *deepening* and the *work*. I only use the Weitzman as a guided meditation, a therapeutic tool, among others, to teach and promote the virtues of deep relaxation and to help a client address certain targeted issues, issues that I strategically planted in previous sessions in the form of non-hypnotic suggestions.

After discussing the two options with Melissa, she decided to start off with the Weitzman Relaxation Induction but didn't rule out attempting a negative visualization at another time. She felt that negative visualization was too direct for her—understandably intimidating--while the Weitzman appeared to be indirect and gentle. I agreed.

The Weitzman Relaxation Induction begins thus:

Sit comfortably in the chair and listen very closely to what I am going to be saying to you. I am going to try a series of experiments on you. Each experiment will be in the form of a question. Each question is either answerable by either "yes" or "no", but it will not be necessary for you to say "yes" or "no" out loud or even perhaps to yourself, because the answer to the question will be your own particular reaction to the question.

The following is an example of the questions asked and how they are composed.

Is it possible for you to allow your eyes to close? (10 second pause)

If they are not yet closed, you may close them now. (5 second pause)

Can you be aware of the point at which the back (of your head) comes in contact with the chair? (10 second pause)

Is it possible for you to imagine the space between your eyes? (10 Second pause)

Can you imagine, now, the distance between your ears?

The "Weitzman" continues at this pace and in this gentle, soothing, inquiring manner for a few more pages. At the mid-point, I asked Melissa how relaxed she was on a one to ten scale. She answered "seven."

I proceeded to deviate from the script by asking her if she "could go back in time and try to imagine, a place that you have been to before or perhaps that brings you inner peace and severity."

A few moments went by and Melissa said, "I can't think of a place."

After a short pause I said, "May I take you to such a place?" I gently asked.

"Yes."

"I will."

I looked to my right, through the wide bay windows that overlooked a quiet country road.

I turned toward Melissa. "Could you imagine yourself sitting on a beach with soft white sand?" (10 second pause).

"Can you imagine running your fingers through soft cool sand?" (10 second pause).

"Can you imagine yourself looking out toward the still, quiet, peaceful body of water beyond the seashore?" (10 second Pause).

"Can you imagine yourself at 32-years-old being at the quiet peaceful seashore, perhaps a breeze of cool air gently blowing through your hair?" (10 second pause).

"Can you imagine yourself at 22-years-old sitting quietly, peacefully, not a care in the world, on the beach, as the sun begins its descent in the sky?" (10 second pause).

"Can you imagine yourself at 12-years-old sitting quietly, peacefully, on the beach, looking out towards the water, and far beyond the light blue horizon?" (10 second pause).

"In your mind's eye can you look gently upon your 12-year-old self and tell her that everything's going to be all right, that she is safe." (15 second pause).

"While you are looking lovingly upon your 12-year-old self, could you please repeat after me?"

Melissa nodded, eyes still closed.

"I will protect you."

"I will protect you. (Five second pause).

"I will nurture you."

"I will nurture you." (Five second pause).

"I will cooperate with you."

"I will cooperate with you." (30 second pause).

"Thank you," I said, indicating that the meditation was over. "You can open your eyes any time you want to."

Melissa opened her eyes and reoriented herself to her surroundings and yawned.

"How was it?"

"Good. Very good," she nodded.

"Any thoughts?"

"Not right now. I need to process it."

"O.K." I smiled. "We'll talk anytime you're ready."

Depending on the client, meditative affirmations can be very helpful, especially if you do them every day for at least a month or more. Meditative affirmations can be a bridge to better mental help or serve to resolve some stubborn self-esteem issues, but there is no evidence that they can cure underlying illnesses or emotional disturbances.

Regarding Melissa, the meditative affirmations that we engaged in, had two main objectives. As mentioned earlier, the meditation was a way for Melissa to safely address her childhood neglect and sexual assault, but equally important, it modeled a way for how she could repair the harm done to her. In his book, *Coming Home: Championing Your Inner Child*, John Bradshaw wisely asserts that an individual in recovery needs to learn how to give themselves what they didn't receive in childhood, as opposed to waiting to receive it from others. Given Melissa's mother's mental health issues, her estrangement from her biological father, and the many stepfathers that went in and out of her life, she couldn't expect the figures in her turbulent childhood to assist in her recovery. Melissa, like many others in her situation, would have to continue to discover ways in which she could grow and develop by cultivating her inner resources.

The months went by uneventfully, then one week, between sessions, Melissa called. She rarely called between sessions. I was sitting in my office chair.

"Hi. Do you have a minute to talk?" Melissa sounded anxious, yet excited at the same time.

"Sure," I replied.

"Something incredible happened."

"Wow." I answered. "What is that?"

"I was at the supermarket with Robert, about to check out and I heard his voice."

"Whose voice?"

"The animal that assaulted me."

"Oh my god."

"Oh my god is right."

"So, what did you do?"

"I carefully turned around to make sure it was him. And it was."

"How did it feel?"

"I was a bit nervous, but I didn't want it to be too obvious because I didn't want Robert to question me, make a commotion, not to make what might happen if I told Robert, it was the guy that assaulted me. So, I asked Robert to get out in front of me to bag the groceries. It was kind of weird standing between the two of them. He was there like any other guy making small talk with the cashier. Since I haven't seen him in well over 22 years, he wouldn't have recognized me."

"How do you feel now?"

"We got home about two hours ago. I feel pretty calm. I was just happy to get out of there. But it seemed so weird that a guy like that appears to be living a normal life. He's apparently oblivious to the kind of awful person he is."

"That's exactly right. When you feel no shame, you do shameful things."

"Exactly." Melissa replied.

In the face of such a strong association to a traumatic event, it would be understandable if Melissa had had a terribly fearful reaction, even a panic attack, if she had had no treatment for post-traumatic stress. Such direct contact with a past assailant, could even result in a dissociative experience and worse yet, a stress related heart attack. But as a result of all the therapeutic hard work she had done, Melissa was literally able to keep "her head about her." Instead of becoming sympathetic nervous system dominant—leading to the activation of her threat detecting amygdala—she was able to think her way through the experience in a self-empowering way.

Epilogue

It wasn't much later, after Melissa's younger son had settled comfortably into kindergarten, that Melissa returned to work, on a part-time basis, taking care of, and becoming a companion to, a disabled elderly woman.

Regarding her weight, after much consultation with her primary care physician and psychiatrist, Melissa went on a strict medically supervised diet and shed 70 pounds over a nine-month period.

I recently heard that the child that started it all, Talbot, now 18, did graduate from high school and enrolled in an engineering program at a local college.

References

Arden, J. (2019) *Mind-Brain-Gene: Toward Psychotherapy Integration.* New York, NY: W. W. Norton.

Bradshaw, J. (1992). *Homecoming: Reclaiming and Healing Your Inner Child.* New York, NY: Random House.

Dubi, M. (2021). Trauma Road Map Series, *Webinar.* https://traumaonline.net/product/trauma-road-map-webinar-series-basic-skills-for-trauma-treatment-jan-13th-2021/

Felitti, V. (2002). The Relationship Between Adverse Childhood Experiences and Adult Health: Turning Gold into Lead, *The Permanente Journal,* Winter 2002.

Peckham, H. (2017) Evolution Perspectives: Attachment theory, affect regulation theory and working with relational trauma. 5(9), *The Neuropsychotherapist Magazine.*

Porges, S. W. (2011) *The Polyvagal Theory: Neurophysiological Foundations of Emotions, Attachment, Communication, and Self-regulation.* New York, NY: W.W. Norton & Company.

Weitzman, B. (1967). The Weitzman Relaxation Induction. Version at: https://www.maryellenmann.com/healingpractices

Winnicott, D.W. (1973). *The Child, the Family, and the Outside World.* Harmondsworth, UK: Penguin.

Carl And Cecilia Revisited

My work with their son Liam had ended years earlier so I was surprised to see their number light up my cell phone screen.

"Roger?"

It was Liam's dad.

"Hi, Carl. How's it going?"

"Good," he answered. "Liam's still thriving. Doing well."

"Great to hear!" I replied.

"I was wondering," Carl continued. "If you might consider seeing me and my wife for counseling?"

I was actually taken aback by his request, but responded positively, nonetheless. "Thanks for the vote of confidence." I replied. "I'll give it some thought. If it's not me, could I recommend a colleague?"

"Sure," Carl replied.

Although Liam's therapy had gone well, I believed that I had made a mistake during a parent consultation about four months into his treatment and still felt the sting of it.

Liam's parents, Carl and Cecilia, had come in to discuss Liam's progress. I had been consulting with Carl monthly but had not yet met Cecilia. Cecilia was director of marketing for a Fortune 500 company and often traveled on business. I was actually surprised to see her sitting next to Carl in my waiting room when I opened my office door.

After some pleasantries and a review of Liam's progress, I asked Cecilia if she could fill me in on her background. Carl had intimated during a previous parent session that Cecilia had "a lot to talk about," but preferred that she provide me with the details of her rather "difficult" childhood in person.

It turned out that Cecilia was the product of at least two generations of severe mental illness. Cecilia's maternal grandmother had been emotionally unstable and physically abusive to her children. Cecilia's mother was diagnosed with schizophrenia in her late twenties, requiring many psychiatric hospitalizations during Cecilia's childhood. As Cecilia related her story, I could see the color gradually drain from her face and her breathing became uneven. "Are you ok?" I offered her a bottle of water.

"I don't feel good," she told her husband. "I have to go."

"Can I help in any way?" I asked.

"I need air. I think I'm going to have a panic attack," she said.

Carl helped Cecilia out of my office and into their car.

A few hours later Carl called me from a nearby emergency room.

"She's stable. I wasn't aware that she had stopped taking her medication. Now she's back on it and is being set up with a psychiatrist."

"Good. Please keep me updated."

I felt awful about what had happened to Cecilia during the session and blamed myself for inadvertently triggering emotionally destabilizing feelings associated with her chaotic childhood. Therapists are supposed to relieve pain not cause it. I vowed to be much more careful in the future.

Like the clients we serve, therapists have feelings, sometimes irrational ones, that have to be carefully examined. The rational part of my brain posited that I wasn't responsible for Cecilia's panic attack. I couldn't have known or anticipated that she had stopped taking her medication (for an anxiety disorder) and consequently would respond so adversely to material that hundreds of clients had shared in my office before without incident. But all that didn't matter. The fact was that she had a panic attack—in my bleeping office!—as a result of the material I had encouraged her to discuss. Cecilia's terrible distress left an indelible impression on my psyche.

After taking the time to reflect on the parenting session with Carl and Cecilia I referred to earlier, I felt comfortable seeing them, since Carl had somewhat reassured me of Cecilia's emotional stability. I also wanted to take advantage of the opportunity to make amends.

Sure enough, a few days later Carl called again to make sure that I remembered that Cecilia had stopped traveling for work and was available most nights and weekends should I decide to take them on as clients.

"Let's try a couple of sessions and see how it goes," I told him. "I'm concerned about how Cecilia reacted to that session we had a few years ago."

"She's much better," Carl replied. "But I hear-ya, man. I hear-ya."

During the first session, by means of getting reacquainted, I went over some identifying data, most of what I already knew. Carl, 43, was a high school English teacher and Cecilia, 38, was working in marketing for a worldwide watch company. They were financially comfortable, had too boys, a 10 and a 12-year-old and liked to travel across the country during the summer to visit relatives in the Carolina's and in upstate New York. Carl's parents were deceased. Cecilia's parents were still alive.

I took some medical history: Carl was on Lipitor for high cholesterol, but otherwise healthy. Cecilia was on Lexapro for anxiety and depression and suffered from lower back pain on and off. Carl and Cecilia reported that they were taking their medication as prescribed by their doctors and were satisfied with the results. Carl and Cecilia both admitted to needing "to shed a few pounds."

"Couldn't we all," I replied.

I took another note or two, looked up from my pad and said.

"I think I have enough information for now. Anything else I should know?"

Carl and Cecilia shook their heads.

"O.K.," I smiled. "So, what brings you in today?"

Carl looked over to Cecilia. "You wanna go first?"

"No, you can go," she replied.

Carl leaned forward and nodded his head affirmatively. "As we discussed before coming here, it's all about honesty," Carl seemed to be addressing both of us, but I remained neutral because in some cases too much "honesty" too early in the therapeutic process could short circuit the treatment and I didn't yet know how much "honesty" Cecilia could actually take.

In the hands of a less experienced or uninformed psychotherapist, Cecilia was vulnerable to being over-exposed to only partly integrated traumatic childhood experiences and was at risk of re-traumatization. It is often the case, that the interventions a psychotherapist chooses to make are just as important as the ones he chooses not to.

"Cecelia gets very reactive and moody, and this creates a tense family atmosphere that's not good for me or the boys." Carl said this in a tempered tone of voice. "I know that she doesn't mean it and it's due to her rough childhood and all, but I'd like to see her work on this, try to make it better, for everyone's sake, including hers." Carl looked over toward his wife.

I nodded and looked at Cecilia. "Any thoughts?"

"He's not entirely wrong. I am emotional. But it's the way he reacts to it. He gets so angry. He'll go days without talking to me. To me I just get it out and it's over with. But it tends to stay with Carl."

Carl responded quickly. "I understand what you're saying. But you won't talk it through. Am I supposed to be happy about that? Just go along as if nothing has happened?"

Cecilia turned away. "I guess that's why we're here," she said half-jokingly, half sarcastically. "Because Carl has to talk everything through."

"That's right, Cecilia. That's right."

Carl had leaned forward and brought his head to his knees. Then he looked up with a comical smile. "Do you think you can help us with this?"

"Yes," I assertively answered. "You both might not get exactly what you want, but I certainly can help."

"Good." Carl smiled.

I responded to Carl and Cecilia quickly to assertively affirm and encourage the robust nature of their exchange and to express how confident I felt in my ability to help them with the communication problem they presented.

The promotion of an open, honest robust dialogue between couples tends to make it easier for them to resolve the communication problems besetting them. In the case of Carl and Cecilia, it was essential. They had apparently endured too many days of tense silence in their marriage, leading to varying degrees of emotional and physical distances between them, rather than the intimacy that they both ostensibly desired. Carl and Cecilia needed to learn how to communicate in ways that respected each other's tolerance for both distance and closeness. Could there be a "sweet spot" for Carl and Cecilia?

The next time I met with Carl and Cecilia I asked, "How did our first session go?"

"Good, " Carl piped up. "It was clarifying. I had never heard Cecilia describe my behavior in such a way. I felt bad about it."

"How about you?" I looked at Cecilia.

"Good." She nodded affirmatively. "I felt validated. I've also felt bad about my behavior and I was relieved not to be judged."

"Wow." I felt excited.

"Speaking of clarification. I wonder if it would be all right if I asked a few questions about your communication. I wasn't sure of one aspect of it."

"Sure," they said in unison.

"Every couple has conflicts," I started. "It's the way they work them out and hopefully resolve them that are the main challenges. But your conflicts too often lead to temporary—and if this is too strong a word, let me know—estrangement."

"Correct." Carl said.

I looked at Cecilia. "Yes. I would agree," she nodded.

"So is it the thing that you're actually having a conflict about or the way in which you talk about the conflict."

Carl and Cecilia were suddenly silent. "That's a good question," Carl said.

"It's a little of both," Cecilia interjected. "But when we go longer periods not speaking it's usually the latter."

"I see," I replied. "Thanks for clearing that up for me."

This clarification was important because I wanted to make sure that they knew that I was clear on the relationship dynamic preventing them from resolving conflicts in a manner satisfying to both of them. It also provided me with a working hypothesis: knowing that Carl was a big believer in talk therapy—he had been in individual therapy when he was younger and was presently in a men's group—that he was probably too often analyzing, out loud, the reason he believed that Cecilia was "reactive" and "moody" and attributing it to Cecilia's adverse childhood experiences, experiences so overwhelming that Cecilia avoided all talk of them.

"Would it be all right Cecilia if you could give me an outline of a conflict between you and Carl that went unresolved and led to temporary estrangement?" I asked.

Carl looked over to Cecilia. "Is that all right?" he asked.

"Well, we're never going to fix this if I don't." Cecilia's tone of voice suggested that she knew that I, and perhaps Carl, were handling her with kid gloves.

"Just last month I reacted strongly to the boys bickering. I just wanted them to shut up. I didn't want them to work out their disagreement. I had had a long day at work, and I just wanted some peace and quiet."

"But you were so caustic with them and dismissive, " Carl responded. "I want our boys to grow up being able to express their feelings."

"All the time?" Cecilia shot back.

"Yes. As long as they're respectful and sensitive to other people."

Carl and Cecilia turned away from each other and attempted to retreat into their respective corners, but I quickly refocused them.

"And then what happened?" I asked. "What happened after the escalation of the conflict over the boys?"

"The boys went to their rooms, and Carl attempted to lecture me on how I should talk to the kids, blah, blah, blah, blah blah. By then I was just shot and went to bed. And a great night was had by all."

"I take it then that a relatively minor conflict turned into a lights-out for everyone."

"Yes," Cecilia answered.

Carl concurred. "That's exactly what happened. The whole night was ruined."

I resisted making an interpretation or providing an in-depth analysis of how and why the conflict described escalated but did want to point out a possible pattern and offer a suggestion before the session ended.

"I can see a pattern of communication between the two of you. Instead of keeping focused on the issue at hand—i.e., the boys noisy bickering—you instead end up analyzing the how's and why's, leading to temporary estrangements? If a conflict arises this week of any kind, you might consider focusing solely on what happened and avoid discussing it in any other way."

"That's all well and good," Carl asserted. "But will it address the underlying problem and prevent future estrangements."

"One step at a time," I replied. "One step at a time."

I opened the next session by asking Carl and Cecilia, "How'd your week go?"

Cecilia looked over to Carl, "Good?"

"Good," Carl concurred.

"Any conflicts?" I asked.

"Yes," Cecilia answered. "But it went well."

"But it was really hard for me," Carl admitted.

"In what way?" I asked.

"It was hard for me not to talk about it afterwards. But I resisted."

"Yeah," Cecilia interjected. "He was coming over to me, but I gave him a look."

"A look?" I smiled.

"Yeah. A look. Like what's up with that. We just talked about this three days ago."

Carl chuckled. "She's right. I can't deny it. She stopped me dead in my tracks."

"Very good," I said. "Very good."

After taking a note or two I looked up from my pad.

"If it's all right Carl I'd like to get an outline of your early life and how you viewed your parents' marriage. Would that be all right?"

"Sure," Carl responded. "Where should I begin?"

"How about where you grew up, how many siblings you had and what family life was like?"

Carl grew up in a working-class suburb of New York City. He was the youngest of three siblings. His father was a mechanic; his mother worked in the lunchroom of a local school.

"When I was 12 or 13, I began to notice that there wasn't much going on between mom and dad, absolutely no affection, not much talk either. My father would sit up late at night watching a ball game and my mother would be in the bedroom drifting off to sleep. This pained and worried me. When I was about to leave for college, I asked my father what was going on between him and mom. He said that their marriage had been dead for quite some time, and there was little hope of changing that. But he assured me that it had nothing to do with me and my brothers and that he'd be here when I returned home from school."

I looked at Carl and nodded sympathetically.

"This is why it's so important to me that me and Cecilia talk things out, stay close. And that the boys grow up in a home that encourages affection and self-expression."

"I can certainly understand where you're coming from, " I replied.

The goal I had in mind for this particular session was for Cecilia to hear why Carl was so invested in open expression between him and Cecilia and the boys. He was fearful of recreating the disengaged aspects of the home he grew up in.

In a touching moment, Cecilia reached over and gently squeezed Carl's hand.

A moment later, Cecilia looked at me and asked, "My turn?"

I tilted my head and said in a comical manner. "I'll have to check my schedule."

We all laughed.

"Don't worry, Roger. I'm not going to fall apart in your office."

I had considered bringing up what had happened at my office a few years before when Cecilia talked about her turbulent childhood, but I had decided out of fear or caution to let that sleeping dog lie.

Cecilia reported that she spent her early childhood down South but moved to New York when her father divorced her mother and won custody of her and her two sisters. Like Carl, Cecilia grew up in a working-class community and during her adolescence and young adulthood endured two stepmothers, the last a critical, fault-finding individual who favored her own children over her and her siblings.

Subsequently, Cecilia opted to graduate from high school a year early and go away to college. She received her first degree in economics and without missing a step completed a master's degree in Business Administration and went to work full time at 23 years old. Although she was financially independent, she remained at home to save money to buy a house. At this point, her stepmother had mellowed some, and she had met Carl. Carl was her one and only boyfriend and love.

"Carl, can you now see why Cecilia has difficulty talking about her early childhood, and how her relationship with two critical, fault finding stepmothers shaped her reactivity and was a problematic model for dialogue and conflict resolution?"

"Yes. But therapy can change that—if you're willing to work it."

"I agree," I said and left it at that.

Now that I had a good picture of Carl's and Cecilia's backgrounds, I wanted to get an accounting of their courtship and early marriage.

Carl took the lead smiling, "We met at school. I was a 28-year-old college senior on the 10-year plan, and she was finishing her masters at 23. It made us a good team, though. An underachiever and an overachiever."

Cecilia chimed in, "Carl was very respectful, very attentive and was willing to travel a far distance to see me during the week and on weekends. I wasn't sure if he would be willing to do that after we finished school. Few guys were willing to do it at all."

"Any particular reason for that?" I asked.

"Well, I was still living at home, going to church on Sundays and kind of saving myself for marriage. It wasn't that I was necessarily against pre-marital sex, but it had to be with the right one."

"What about you Carl? What were your thoughts on the matter?"

"I actually liked that about Cecilia. Since I had not had any success in relationships the other way around, why not try it differently. I even started going to church with Cecilia and her family."

Carl and Cecilia married two years later and four years into their marriage had borne two children. When Carl achieved tenure as a schoolteacher, they decided to purchase a house in a more affluent community than they both grew up in. Carl and Cecilia thrived in their respective careers and the boys were doing well. When Cecilia began to travel for work, Carl managed the boys and the household. What could be wrong?

"Did Cecilia's travel affect your relationship?" I asked.

By this point in the therapy, I was working on a second hypothesis: that Cecilia's travel kept Carl and Cecilia's communication and other troubling marital issues at bay because they were with each other less frequently. Once Cecilia stopped traveling for work and was home more, their difficulties being a couple became less tolerable.

"We certainly missed Cecilia, but since I had such a good schedule—home by 2, summers and holidays off, it was a sacrifice worth making for Cecilia's career."

"What about you Cecilia? How did it work out for you?"

Cecilia was suddenly quiet, still. She looked down, inhaled, and said.

"I didn't particularly like the travel or the work I was doing, and I missed being home."

Cecilia paused again and seemed on the verge of sharing something important. She turned to Carl and said, "You said that you wanted honesty, right?"

Carl nodded. "Say what you got-ta say."

"Well, since I stopped traveling, it's been a big disappointment for me. I like being with the boys and all—don't get me wrong—but I thought our marriage would be different, sort of renewed."

"In what way?" I asked.

And here came the curve ball.

"Well, when Carl and I have these conflicts, *estrangements*, there's no sex. It's as if he's not attracted to me at all."

"Is that true, Carl? I mean about the attractiveness?"

"Yes and no," Carl's tone of voice was defensive. "When we have these disputes—it could be between her and I or her and the boys—and she won't hash them out, won't talk-—I just don't feel loving toward her in that way. I'll help her pack her clothes for a trip, make sure she has a cup of coffee for her long drive to work, even kiss her good-bye, but not that."

"How come?" I asked.

"Because that's something special. It shouldn't be taken lightly."

"What are your thoughts, Cecilia?"

"For me sex is a strong biological and an emotional need. It really makes me feel good and relaxed and more at ease for days after. I feel that I really missed out because I don't want to talk through things endlessly with Carl and unearth the reasons for my emotional outbursts."

"Would you agree that your perspective on sex has grown or always was different than Carl's?"

"Yes." Cecilia responded.

"Were you aware of this, Carl?"

"No. This is the first time I've heard it in that way."

I let Cecilia and Carl's words linger for a while.

"There are many ways of being intimate," I began. "Perhaps a discussion about your sex life, your respective needs and beliefs can be a model for talking about sex and other things."

"I'll certainly give it a try," Cecilia sounded pessimistic.

"This is the first time I've heard this, " Carl was shaking his head.

I got the sense that Carl wanted to talk more about Cecilia, but I decided not to indulge him.

"I lot of important things were said today by both of you. Give it some time to sink in. Then talk about it at home. We'll pick it up next week."

The next session Carl and Cecilia broached the subject of their sexual relationship at the outset.

"We had a good discussion," Carl offered. "I now realize that Cecilia's feelings toward sex were similar to mine when it came to pre-marriage, but that's where the similarities stopped. To me it continued to be a special experience guided by religious teachings, an honest expression of love between two married people, not a need."

I looked at Cecilia. "I take responsibility for not communicating my feelings after we got married and had children, " she said. "I thought Carl's not pressing me to have sex when we met, traveling long distances to see me after we graduated from school, was endearing, so I just went along. And now I feel that I just missed out."

"Missed out on what?" I asked.

"You know—the whole glory of it—your young body, your beauty. Look at me now." Cecilia stretched out her arms.

"You're beautiful," Carl retorted. "I love your body."

The early days of a blossoming love and the sexual interludes that often follow are sensations that bring the body to life in ways it had never experienced before, transforming, deeply affecting, unforgettable. It was obvious that Cecilia believed that she had missed out on such a transformation and no revival of her sexual relationship with Carl could retrieve it.

I was saddened by Cecilia's resignation and had the urge to reassure her, to tell her that life was full of surprises, even in the sexual realm.

Then I had an intuition and pulled out a small pad from my little side table.

Stealing a move from a colleague who was a sex therapist, I put pen to pad and scribbled. *"Sensual body message every other day leading to orgasm or no. Make it work."* I handed the script to Carl.

Carl looked it over once or twice and handed it to Cecilia.

"Me to her?" Carl asked.

"You to her and her to you."

"No matter how I feel?"

"No matter how you feel." I was unequivocal.

"Ok," Carl said with a perplexed laugh.

"Thank you," Cecilia said this softly, almost in audibly.

During the session, when Cecilia so movingly related the feeling of lost opportunity to bring her body to life, I realized that she was not talking about sex per se, but more broadly about her deep need for positive and yet pleasurable sensory experiences.

It is safe to assume, that during her infancy and early childhood Cecilia was deprived of the positive sensory input that all human beings need during development to learn how to effectively process and manage feeling states and regulate them. Her mother's psychiatric hospitalizations and her emotionally unstable grandmother's inability to step in and provide Cecilia and her sister with loving attachments left a gaping hole in her emotional development.

Although Carl's role model for marriage and family life turned dour as his parent's relationship became more and more remote, Carl and his brother received more than their share of "good enough" parenting from his mother and grandmother from the moment he was born. These early positive experiences and the absence of the chaos brought on by severe mental illness, allowed Carl to be open and receptive to talk therapy, resilient and positive about healing even the deepest emotional wounds.

In light of these differences between Carl and Cecilia, I concluded that Carl was emotionally stronger than Cecilia and could more easily take on the burden of the kind of change that Cecilia wanted and badly needed in their marriage, but that Cecilia couldn't necessarily, at this time or in the near future, shoulder the burden of excavating her past and analyzing the relationship between her emotional reactivity and her tumultuous and *traumatic* childhood. This was not another working hypothesis. This was a conviction.

The following session Carl and Cecilia reported that they were able to give each other sensual massages but with some strategic difficulty.

"The kids are used to us always being around, so it was hard to make time, particularly with our schedules. We get up early, so we're usually asleep by 10."

I would have none of it. "Meet at a hotel before you get home from work if you have to. Your marriage depends on it."

Carl laughed. "What about the kids?"

"Pay someone to come over to help them with their homework or drive them somewhere."

"They would love that," Cecilia said with enthusiasm. "And I would too."

I looked at Carl. "Agreed?"

"Agreed." Carl said this with conviction.

I took out my pad and wrote out another script.

Two sensual massages, one sexual interlude.

I handed the script to Carl. He smiled and handed to Cecilia.

"This is not going to be easy," Carl said.

I looked directly at Cecilia. "Make three dates with him."

"I will." There was a glint in Cecilia's eyes.

The next week Carl and Cecilia reported that they were able to work out a routine—so the change wasn't so obvious—that they would give each other the massages before bedtime and have the sexual interlude before a slightly later dinner, "nap time" to the boys.

I commended them on their ingenuity. "Us busy older folk need to have dates that we stick to, to enjoy the grander pleasures in life."

"Well said," Carl piped in.

"It was my pleasure sir, madame." I said with an affected English accent.

We all laughed.

"So, how does it feel?" I asked them.

"Carl's a very good lover, "Cecilia asserted. Carl's face turned a shade of red. "He knows his way around pretty good."

"An invaluable skill," I replied.

The next script I offered had a slight change in instruction.

Two sexual interludes and one sensual massage.

For several weeks Carl and Cecilia were able to have consistent and mutually satisfying sensual and sexual interludes of varying kinds. One weekend they arranged for the boys to spend a few nights with Carl's brother and wife and spent the time in an upstate hotel enjoying rich foods and the sensations brought on by the continued exploration of each other's bodies.

Around the tenth session, Carl reached over and took Cecilia's hand.

"How's it going between us?" he asked.

"Good," Cecilia nodded. "Good."

"You're happy with our love making?"

"Yes," Cecilia replied. For a moment I thought Carl was going to propose to her again, ask to reaffirm their vows.

"So, do you think we could talk about your reactivity and how it relates to your past?"

"I think I'm better," Cecilia said.

"Yes. You are. But I just don't want it to rare back up."

Cecilia looked down, then up at me.

"Carl," I interjected. "I think what you've been doing is great, being a loving—in all ways—patient, considerate husband."

"He has," Cecilia concurred.

"And what you are providing your wife through your love making is the type of positive sensory experiences she never had as a child and longed for as an adult. You are providing the circumstances for her growth sexually and emotionally. Perhaps there will come a day when Cecilia is ready, able, willing and most importantly, *wanting* to examine her past and see how it relates to the present. But it is my considered professional opinion that this is not the time."

"I'd be lying if I said I wasn't disappointed, but I respect your opinion."

Cecilia reached over and took Carl's hand. "Maybe one day. Don't give up hope."

Two sessions later the therapy ended.

———

Nearly a year and the half past and I hadn't heard from either Carl or Cecilia. Then one afternoon, on a lunch break, I got out of my car and I heard my name called. At first, I couldn't recognize the couple who had emerged from a nearby Mercedes Benz.

"Roger—"

I peered into the couple's faces as if I was near sighted.

It was Carl and Cecilia. "Hey guys," I finally said, shaking their outstretched hands. "How are you? How's my boy Liam?"

"We're great." Larry said proudly. "Thank you. Thank you for all your help."

Carl and Cecilia had lost as much as 40 or 50 pounds, were trim, firm and beaming with vitality. I noticed that they were heading towards the gym.

"Have a good work out," I called over my shoulder.

Carl smiled back at me and gave me a thumbs up!

The striking physical changes in Carl and Cecilia, the vitality of their physiques and the spring in their step, reminded me of the scene at the end of the movie *Back To The Future* when Marty McFly returns from the past to encounter his completely transformed father and mother George and Lorraine, all dapper and flirtatious, opening a recently delivered box containing copies of George's first sci-fi novel.

Life is certainly full of second chances, for clients and therapists as well.

Additional Reading

Retraumatization: Assessment, Treatment, and Prevention, Edited By Melanie P. Duckworth, Victoria M. Follette, 2012, Routledge

The Science of Couples Therapy with Peter Janetzki, Science Of Psychotherapy Podcast 7, September 24, 2018. Retrieved from https://www.thescienceofpsychotherapy.com/sop-7-the-science-of-couples-therapy-with-peter-janetzki/

Rebuilding The Brain With Psychotherapy, Savita Malhotra, Swapnajeet Sahoo, *Indian Journal of Psychiatry*, 2018.

Adverse Child Experience Survey, (ACE), CDC-Kaiser Permanente ACE study, 1998.

When Therapists Make Mistakes, Dr. Keely Kolmes, drkkolmes.com, August 10, 2009.

"We Are More than Our Parents' Mental Illness: Narratives from Adult Children, International Journal of Environmental Journal of Environmental Research and Public Health, 16(5): 839 March 2019.

TREATMENT OF A 12-YEAR-OLD BOY WITH TRAUMA

When Colin was 10 years old, he was told that he had diabetes. In retrospect, his symptoms leading up to his diagnosis made complete sense, but since he had such a full, busy schedule, his parents and paediatrician believed that he was merely over-tired and needed some rest. But when Colin began to lose weight and muscle mass, his parents became alarmed and brought him to his doctor.

"You have diabetes," the doctor blurted out. "Your blood sugar is so high I can't believe you're even standing." Colin stood in stunned silence, unable to process what he was being told.

The doctor ushered Colin's parents into the room. "His blood sugar is dangerously high. He needs to go to emergency."

That is how Colin and his parents learned that he had a chronic life-threatening illness. To him and his parents it was all so unreal.

Two years after his initial diagnosis of diabetes, Colin's parents came to see me for a consultation to discuss their son's increasing feelings of anxiety and depression— feelings that Colin and his parents attributed to the stress associated with the management of his diabetes. Although Colin's distress was related to his illness, I did a detailed social, developmental, and medical history even before discussing the presenting problem, all the while giving his parents the opportunity to get a sense of what I was like so that they could decide whether they wanted me to work with their son.

It turned out that Colin was an exceptional 12-year-old, achieving at high levels in all areas of his life. He was an A student, a competitive swimmer, an artist, and he had a busy social life. Other than the diabetes, his medical history was uneventful. He usually had a good appetite, slept soundly through the night, and responded well to physical affection. He made appropriate eye contact when spoken to. He was polite and courteous, and respectful toward his elders. Colin got along with everyone who came into his orbit.

But during the unstructured periods of his day, Colin was feeling increasingly anxious and depressed, and some of the more pleasurable methods of relieving his symptoms (such as video-game playing, skate boarding, or shooting hoops in the backyard) had lost their effectiveness. Colin's new pediatrician offered a trial of antidepressant medication to treat his symptoms, but he and his parents decided to try therapy instead.

Colin presented as a tall, thin and lanky boy with a somewhat pale and drawn complexion. His parents introduced him to me, and we shook hands. A few minutes later he told them that they could wait outside the room until the session was over. I reached behind my side table and raised a soft squishy round ball above my head. "Catch?" I smiled.

"Sure!" Colin laughed as if he was caught off guard.

"Tell me about your day. From the moment you wake up until you go to sleep."

As we tossed the ball back and forth, Colin filled me in. "On school days I get up about 7:30, check my levels, and have something to eat. I get dressed, pack my lunch, make sure my insulin pump and pack are right, and catch the bus at 8:30."

Colin went on to tell me that most school days went smoothly—he liked his teachers and enjoyed his special subjects, especially art and woodwork.

"Three nights a week I swim with the team and one night I have an art lesson."

"How often do you compete?"

"We have meets every couple of weeks." Colin's parents had told me that the swim meets often involved early morning travel on weekends and they asked him if he wanted to take a break from it, but Colin declined because he loved being on the team.

"Most weekend nights I do homework and assignments, watch some TV, take a shower, and head off to bed," Colin concluded.

"Thanks for filling me in," I smiled.

During our next two sessions, I sought the answer to two important questions regarding having a chronic (although manageable) disease. Did Colin accept his diabetes, and did he feel confident in his self-care?

"I do accept it, but I'm hopeful that there will be a cure one day. I think I manage it pretty well, although checking my levels and adjusting what I eat is annoying. I get frustrated at times."

"Have you had a scare in the past year and a half, regarding your sugar levels or your health?'

"No," Colin replied.

"Sounds like you've got things under control," I replied. "And I too hope that there is a cure one day."

At the next session I checked in with Colin on how well our sessions were going for him. He said he felt comfortable and positive. I then proceeded to review with him what he had told me the previous two sessions about his full and busy life and his acceptance and management of his diabetes. He reaffirmed that it was manageable.

Consequently, I felt confident about my next intervention.

"But I was wondering," I offered, "Why then do you think you're feeling anxious and depressed?"

Colin looked away. "I don't know." Tears welled up in his eyes. He removed his glasses and wiped his face.

Minutes later, Colin looked up at me, his weary brown eyes seeking an answer.

I leaned forward and gently asked, "Do you think you might be able to describe what happened in the doctor's office when he told you that you had diabetes? Whatever you can remember."

Colin nodded. "I can remember it like it was yesterday." I waited.

"He said my blood sugar was so high he couldn't believe I was standing. And he blurted out that I had diabetes! Just like that. When he told my parents, they turned white."

I shook my head.

Since I was working on the hypothesis that Colin's experience in the doctor's office was likely a traumatic one, I did not encourage him to tell me more than he had already offered for fear of re-traumatizing him by over-exposing him to too much traumatic energy so early in the therapy. But I did feel confident enough to do some cognitive work.

"How do you think the doctor should have handled it?"

"Not like that," Colin asserted. "He should have been calmer, more reassuring."

"You're exactly right, "I replied. "I've had several colleagues in a similar situation, and they handled it a lot differently. They would have told you that they were concerned about your blood sugar reading and brought your parents in. They would have calmly but firmly instructed your parents that you needed to get to the nearest emergency department."

"That would have been better." The color had returned to Colin's face.

We sat in silence for a while. Then I proceeded to do more cognitive work. "You know, Colin, that doctor appeared to panic, and he handled the situation poorly. For all we know *his* blood sugar was up, and *he* was having a stressful day." We both chuckled. "But nonetheless, from a purely medical point of view, his doctoring was right on the mark. He got you out of his office quickly and straight to emergency so you could get proper care."

"I can see that," Colin shook his head in agreement.

Doing cognitive work in trauma therapy is important. It not only serves to elucidate partial misinterpretations or "take-aways" from the traumatic event but can simultaneously loosen up or safely defuse traumatic energies lodged in the autonomic nervous system. In Colin's case, presenting a more balanced, *more realistic*, picture of what happened in the doctor's office is a good example of this. In some cases, the client's misinterpretations of a traumatic event can be dissociative, requiring more time to carefully examine and reconstruct.

At the following session, I reviewed with Colin the material we had previously covered and asked if it had been helpful. "Yes," he replied. "I feel less shaky."

"Good."

I grabbed the ball from behind my side table and threw it to him. He smiled broadly, red cheeks and all.

"Today I would like to talk about triggers," I continued. "What causes you to become overly anxious?"

Colin gave it some thought. "It's when my levels spike despite my best effort." "OK," I nodded affirmatively. "I'll teach you some relaxation techniques to reduce your anxiety. Anybody can use them; all you need is a brain!" Colin laughed out loud.

I proceeded to demonstrate a few easy breathing exercises: the limp noodle (where the client bends over and goes limp and holds the position for one or two minutes), mindful focused breathing, and a form of breathing that initiates self-hypnosis. I also told him that sucking on peppermints, pressing a small cold bottle of water against his forehead, or counting backwards from a hundred by threes were also ways to signal to your brain to relax. I did not want to complicate matters by explaining to Colin that all these anxiety-reducing offerings were evidenced-based methods of transitioning from the sympathetic (all feeling and dysregulation) to the parasympathetic (calm and equilibrium) nervous-system branches within the autonomic nervous system.

Before the session came to an end, I gave Colin some therapeutic homework. I asked him to consider describing in verbal, narrative, or pictorial form what happened in the doctor's surgery after he was told that he had diabetes. "This would be for a future session," I explained. The focus on triggers and the introduction of relaxation techniques to address them was a way to help Colin take control of his anxiety in the here and now and prepare him to deal with and process much more emotionally intense material in the future.

The next week Colin came in and said that he had practiced some of the relaxation techniques and they were helpful. He especially liked the limp noodle because it approximated the way in which he rotated his shoulders and bent his upper body over the lip of the pool at swim meets. Colin added that counting by threes backward from a hundred was also effective.

"The counting promotes deliberate thinking," I told him.

Deliberate thinking exercises wed the parasympathetic nervous system to the neocortex, the part of the brain where reason resides.

Colin offered to verbally describe what happened after the doctor told him he had diabetes.

"I was put on the examining table and was hydrated with an intravenous line. An ambulance came and took me to the hospital. I continued on fluids for a while longer and eventually was given insulin."

"How did that go?"

"I was really scared at first, but as I began to feel better, more like my old self, I began to settle down."

"How were you treated in the hospital?

"Good. Everyone was great. For three days my parents never left my side."

Once again I reinforced the positive elements of his experience at the doctor's office and at the hospital. I encouraged him to talk them over with his parents as well. Through the reinterpretation of these experiences, I was hopeful that Colin would emotionally internalize a more balanced and realistic perspective and supplant the traumatic belief system that fuelled the traumatic energy that had been lodged in his body for two years.

During the next few sessions Colin and I practiced the relaxation techniques I had introduced earlier in the therapy and continued to review the new ways in which he was conceiving his experiences at the doctor's and at the hospital that had occurred two years earlier. We agreed to meet again after he returned from a two-week family vacation and the start of a new school year in September.

After Labor Day, I texted Colin's father about setting up our next appointment. I waited for his reply with great anticipation. I was looking forward to resuming my work with this exceptional young man.

Colin's father called me that night. "Colin says that he's feeling really good. He's using the techniques you taught him and doesn't think he needs to come in anymore. He told me to tell you thanks for all your help."

"Terrific," I said, even though I was deflated over his decision to discontinue the therapy. "Tell him to have a great school year!"

Case considerations. Colin had a "lower-case" traumatic experience; it was much easier to treat than a capital "T" trauma. Colin was also experiencing puberty, and his increased anxiety was a result of hormonal turbulence. He simply needed to give shape and order to his experience at the doctor's and the hospital to move on emotionally.

When I contacted Colin's parents to get their permission to write this case study, they told me that Colin was doing great. "He's never been better."

***

Starting conversations with children

There are numerous ways that conversations can be started with children, ranging from simple narratives about themselves and their activities to asking them to use their skills of observation and deduction. These are examples of simple, but effective prompts:

1. A straightforward request: "Tell me about your day from start to finish."

2. Imagine if: "What would you do if you were given two thousand dollars a week for the rest of your life to live on? What would you do with it?"

3. Detective work: my office window overlooks a parking lot with

several stores: "The person or persons who just got out of their car—what store do you think they're going to?"

The third example is especially helpful for children on the autistic spectrum to teach them forms of symbolism—older people might be going to their local coffee shop, people who are more "dressed-up" to the high-end restaurant, and tradesmen to the deli. We observe their ages, clothes, the way they are walking; where they're parked; and, of course, what kind of car they're driving.

There are other avenues from different cultures that can open the channels for conversation. Many cultures use some form of a "talking stick" that empowers the holder both to have the right to speak and to have some feeling of control in the conversation.

They may choose to speak or to just hand the stick on—either action involves the child directly in the conversational experience. Children who pass the stick on may be more comfortable speaking the next time they are handed the stick (Mehl-Madrona & Mainguy, 2014).

Counsellors and therapists who work with children will benefit from exploring the many ways in which conversations with children can be encouraged, including online (e.g., "Helping Children Talk," 2017).

It is equally important to know how to be sensitive when children are not ready to talk.

Cognitive work

Traumatic experiences often result in cognitive misinterpretations that become the implicit message (or subconscious "take-away") of the event. This is related to retention of emotional memory in the limbic area, particularly the amygdala, of highly charged events that trigger the sympathetic nervous system (Clark, 1995). For example, if parents must leave a child in hospital overnight, and the child is traumatized by the medical procedures, this may cause a negative phobic adaptation toward doctors and nurses that can manifest in certain behaviors later in life. The implicit retention of this misinterpretation or dysfunctional take-away—that doctors and nurses are in some way bad—is related to the body's memory of the catastrophic events and the distress of abandonment. This needs to be addressed and a positive reinterpretation introduced. In severe cases, there may need to be a process of de-association of the event from the many connections that may have been created over time before deeper trauma work can be begin. J. Eric Gentry addresses this issue in his book, *Forward-*

Facing Trauma Therapy (Compassion Unlimited, 2016).

Thinking deliberately

Deliberate thinking has been shown to reduce anxiety by calming the amygdala in response to increased activity in the prefrontal cortex and the cingulate gyrus. Deliberate thinking reduces the amount of fantasy and imaginative wandering. Research on mind wandering has provided a surprising amount of information on the process of deliberate thinking on the basis of an "either/or" neural contingency (Fox & Christoff, 2018).

Increasing focus on deliberate thought is another way of calming the emotional centers of the brain and increasing the sense of safety and feeling of comfort in the therapeutic, conversational process. Edward de Bono describes effective thinking as beneficial for self-empowerment and building self-esteem (de Bono, 2014). Asking someone to think deliberately about something, as suggested in the examples above, can disrupt the negative process of ruminating on problems and difficulties.

Capital "T" trauma and lower-case "t" trauma

Capital "T" traumas are usually caused by severe events, such as life-threatening confrontations, and have a single event catastrophic impact on the autonomic nervous system, causing a high degree of emotional dysregulation in the form of post-traumatic stress symptoms.

Lower-case "t" traumas can occur over time and are usually of less intense impact. Growing up in an unstable home due to financial stressors, alcoholism of a parent, or the mental illness of a sibling can cause lower-case traumas. "Post-traumatic-like" behaviors of parents or grandparents, inadvertently passed on to their offspring, or constant exposure to media coverage of terrorism, can also be sources of lower-case "t" traumas.

Both types of trauma result in emotional dysregulation and an inability to sustain periods of calm or relaxation without assistance or unhealthy symptom reduction such as alcohol consumption and/or drug use. Peter Levine describes a series of gentle, self-nurturing exercises to treat trauma pockets in the body in his book *Healing Trauma: A Pioneering Program for Restoring the Wisdom of Your Body* (Sounds True, 2008).

For more information, see Barbash (2017).

References

Barbash, E. (2017, March 13). The different kinds of trauma: Small "t" versus large "T".
Psychology Today. Retrieved from https://www.psychologytoday.com/au/blog/trauma-and-hope/201703/different- types-trauma-small-t-versus-large-t

Clark, G. A. (1995). Emotional learning: Fear and loathing in the amygdala. *Current Biology, 5*, 246–248. doi:10.1016/S0960-9822(95)00050-9

De Bono, E. (2014). Deliberate thinking: The most important human resource. Retrieved from https://www.debono.com/deliberate-thinking/

Ecker, B. (2015, January). Understanding memory reconsolidation. *The Neuropsychotherapist, 10*, 4–22.

Fox, K., & Christoff, K. (Eds.). (2018). *The Oxford handbook of creative thought: Mind- wandering, creativity, and dreaming.* Oxford, United Kingdom: Oxford University Press.

Gentry, J. E. (2016). *Forward-facing trauma therapy: Healing the moral wound.* Sarasota, FL: Compassion Unlimited.

Helping children talk about difficult topics. (2017, June 13). Retrieved from https://developingminds.net.au/articles-for-professionals/2017/6/13/helping- children-talk-about-difficult-topics

Mehl-Madrona, L., & Mainguy, B. (2014). Introducing healing circles and talking circles into primary care. *The Permanente Journal, 18*(2), 4–9.

Szasz,T. (2003). The psychiatric protection order for the "battered mental patient". *BMJ, 327*, 1449–1451.

White, M. (2005). Children, trauma and subordinate storyline development. *The International Journal of Narrative Therapy and Community Work, 3–4*, 10–21.

ABOUT THE AUTHOR

Roger Keizerstein, LCSW, is a child psychotherapist and a certified clinical trauma professional. He has been in private practice in East Setauket, NY, for 38 years. His stories and essays have appeared in *Newsday*, *The New York Times*, *The Southampton Press*, *Listen Magazine*, *The Neuropsychotherapist,* and *The Science of Psychotherapy*. He lectures on trauma and post-traumatic stress throughout the New York metropolitan area.